ANITA BARTHOLOMEW

SIEGE

An American Tragedy

This book is dedicated to the law enforcement officers who defended the Capitol despite being greatly outnumbered and subjected to grievous injuries and abuse.

The republic you helped save that day owes you its gratitude.

"One does not establish a dictatorship in order to safeguard a revolution; one makes the revolution in order to establish the dictatorship."

— George Orwell, 1984

Contents

1

Foreshadowing

*"Just say that the election was corrupt
and leave the rest to me and the Republican congressmen."*

— Then-President Donald Trump to Department of Justice officials

On November 15, 2020, Fox News host Maria Bartiromo had some shocking revelations to share with her *Sunday Morning Futures* viewers.

According to her featured guest, Rudy Giuliani, former New York City Mayor and current personal attorney for President Donald J. Trump, something had gone very wrong in the recent presidential election. And it hadn't happened by chance. Giuliani made the connection between rampant vote tampering in the presidential election and a software company with businesses in Cuba—and links to China.

When Giuliani appeared on screen, he dropped another bombshell: Smartmatic software was designed by and for none other than the late socialist president of Venezuela, Hugo Chavez.

"And this company has tried-and-true methods for fixing elections," he explained, "by calling a halt to the voting when you're running too far behind."

While that was sinking in, Bartiromo showed her audience a graphic that indicated Smartmatic software was used on voting machines in the swing states of Arizona, Georgia, Michigan, Nevada, Pennsylvania, and Wisconsin. Smartmatic was also, she claimed, the owner of Dominion Voting Systems.

As regular Fox viewers probably knew by then, Dominion Voting Systems was one of the top voting technology purveyors in the US.

If true, this intel was beyond damning. It was explosive. It could offer the proof that Trump had been right all along: the election had been rigged. And foreign nationals—socialists and communists—had been involved in the rigging.

The only problem? Almost none of what Bartiromo and Giuliani stated with such authority was accurate. Though its owners were Venezuelan nationals, Smartmatic was an American election software company. It didn't own the entirely separate electronic voting machine maker Dominion Voting Systems. It had no businesses in Cuba. It had no known links to China.

But even if all of what Bartiromo and Giuliani alleged that morning about Smartmatic were accurate, it couldn't have changed the outcome of the 2020 presidential election.

In all of the United States, Smartmatic software was used in a single county only: reliably Democratic Los Angeles, California, which hadn't been won by a Republican presidential candidate since Ronald Reagan in 1984.

None of that mattered. The disinformation campaign narrative that originated with Trump loyalists like Giuliani, and was being promoted unskeptically by friendly media, was as riveting as any spy thriller.

Trump and his allies would eventually claim that a massive conspiracy cost Trump seven states — the six in Bartiromo's graphic plus New Mexico—that he'd actually won. And the accusations went beyond vote-switching election software and machines to include fake registrations, counterfeit ballots, illegal votes by hordes of undocumented immigrants, votes cast mysteriously by long-dead citizens, and legal ballots discarded.

Who could be trusted any more?

County employees who mailed out and processed registration forms would have to have been in on it. Election workers who counted the ballots? At least some of them would have had to know. Not even those friendly seniors who came out of retirement each year to man the polling stations on election day were above suspicion. Judges, postal workers, printers, Democratic politicians at every level of government, all were targeted as co-conspirators. As the campaign to persuade voters that their votes had been stolen continued, Trump loyalists would add more conspirators to the list. The CIA. Foreign operatives in Italy and Spain. And that amorphous amalgam of faceless bureaucrats known as the "Deep State."

Pundits in the Fox media empire, throughout Trump's presidency, had regularly lent credence to Trump's positions and rhetoric on virtually every topic. It was the most watched cable TV news network in the United States. There was probably no better place to sow seeds of fear and doubt, and hope they would spread like kudzu.

Nevermind that Dominion was also among the major voting technology companies in 2016—the year Trump actually won the presidency. Nevermind that other Republicans had won races in the 2020 election.

Claims of election fraud by those in the Trump universe were also being telegraphed to the far fringes of the web. There, the allegations expanded, morphed, and got molded into dark fables too preposterous and paranoid for even the most evil of Marvel Comics super-villains. Most in non-Fox mainstream media didn't immediately seem to grasp that such blatant nonsense would stick. If they took note at all, it was to point fingers and chuckle.

By four days after the election, although several states had not yet been officially called, it was clear that Trump had indeed lost. It would soon become apparent that former Vice President Joseph Biden had won the popular vote by more than seven-million and the electoral college vote by seventy-four. Yet, Trump insisted that he, not Biden, had actually won "by a lot," suggesting, like his personal attorney, Rudy Giuliani, that Biden was attempting a coup against the rightful president.

Trump announced that Giuliani would give a press conference on November 7, 2020, at the Four Seasons, to update everyone on their plans for legal challenges.

Anyone reading the announcement assumed that meant Philadelphia's posh Four Seasons Hotel. A clarification soon appeared: the press conference would be in the parking lot of the Four Seasons Total Landscaping Company, an unassuming business in an industrial part of Philadelphia, Pennsylvania. Reporters who attended gleefully pointed out that the venue was across the street from a crematorium and down the block from where the Fantasy Island sex shop was running a "Dildo Madness" sale.

Giuliani seemed almost pitiful as he insisted Trump had won, nevermind the vote count that said otherwise. He alleged that ballot boxes in Pennsylvania had been stuffed with the votes of dead people. He promised lawsuits. In the midst of all this, word came out that the Associated Press had just called Pennsylvania for Joe Biden. Someone in the crowd yelled, "Go home. The game is over."

Reporters began leaving before the press conference ended. Although Nevada, Arizona, and Georgia had yet to be called (and all three would go to Biden), Pennsylvania's twenty electoral votes gave Biden the two-hundred-seventy he needed to win, plus three to spare. Case closed.

Or so most of the world believed at that moment.

But even as members of the media who'd shown up for the event smirked, packed up, and moved on, a significant portion of the population still took Trump at his word and, by extension, Rudy Giuliani. It was on the news—the news they watched, anyway—so it couldn't easily be dismissed. Their claims of massive irregularities and rigging rang true to followers. Unlike the "elites" who ridiculed Giuliani's choice of venue, the average Joe and Jane probably tuned in and saw a place that looked much like the businesses where they worked. Rather than making him look pitiful, it could have suggested that Giuliani was a regular guy, like his boss. Like them.

On November 19, 2020, four days after his appearance on Bartiromo's show, Giuliani gave another press conference, more comical—at least, to most of the world—than the Four Seasons Landscaping fiasco. Distracting from his insistence that the evidence showed massive election fraud, a line of hair dye melted off his sweaty sideburns and trickled down his cheek. Undeterred, perhaps unaware, he continued:

> "This pattern repeats itself in a number of states, almost exactly the same pattern... which suggests that there was a plan, from a centralized place, to execute these various acts of voter fraud, specifically focused on big cities, and specifically focused on, as you would imagine, big cities controlled by Democrats."

Appearing along with him, former federal prosecutor and current defense attorney Sidney Powell, repeated the allegations of a much wider conspiracy, and included billionaire George Soros into the mix of Chinese, Cuban, and Venezuelan conspirators.

Fact-checkers and reporters for most of the mainstream media immediately debunked this as baseless nonsense. What few knew at the time was that the Trump campaign, itself, in a comprehensive fourteen-page memo, had *already* debunked all these claims almost a week prior to the press conference. If Trump's followers had known, would it have mattered?

His truest believers believed in him utterly. Trump came across as a guy who didn't put up with anyone's bullshit. His fans mistook that trait for honesty, though it was anything but. His willingness to break presidential norms was breathtaking.

Shamelessness was his super-power.

Some pundits, like liberal commentator Rachel Maddow, intimated he was in Putin's pocket. But he didn't necessarily want to aid Putin. He wanted to be Putin. He had an affinity for despots. When, in 2018, the Chinese communist party eliminated term limits, making it possible for Xi Jinping to serve as president for life, Trump praised the Chinese president and the party's decision, musing at a closed-door fundraiser, "Maybe we'll have to give that a shot someday." The country was accustomed to the outrageous from Trump but still, he had to be joking, right? The Trump White House wouldn't say.

The only reasonable expectation one could have of Trump was that he would never be reasonable, unless reasonableness somehow advanced his self-interest. Giving up the power of the presidency certainly wouldn't have done that, so why would anyone imagine that losing an election would persuade Trump to walk away willingly?

And he might not have had to, at least not in 2021, if not for the Covid-19 pandemic.

As the contagion first spread across the county in early 2020, state and local governments tried to control it by closing all but essential businesses. The jobs of many of those whose work could not be done from home disappeared. Their businesses languished. Meanwhile, white-collar workers, untethered from the office but still earning the same salaries when working remotely, competed in bidding wars for houses with home offices and manicured acreage—their wealth increasing even while they slept, thanks to 401Ks invested in a stock market propped up by Federal Reserve policies.

Service and blue collar workers and business owners who were deemed non-essential, sidelined by stay-at-home orders, worried about paying rents, mortgages, and other bills. It didn't matter if a virus was to blame. Who could vent their angst at a bit of barely alive biological matter? Frustration and rage needed human targets: governors and mayors who were keeping them from earning a decent living, and "elites" who never felt the pinch. Suspicions percolated. Was the virus's risk overblown? Worse, was it all just a hoax, some devious plan to control people and limit their freedom?

Was it, as Trump had hinted, part of a scheme to bring him down?

Trump had his own reasons for downplaying the seriousness of Covid-19, but he echoed demands to cancel governors' stay-at-home orders. And his attitude emboldened his followers. If the president didn't take the virus so seriously, should they?

With no good treatments, and no vaccines, as yet, governors increased restrictions to decrease the spread. Meanwhile, Trump's all-caps tweets told the skeptical and downright suspicious that he was on their side:

"LIBERATE MINNESOTA."

"LIBERATE MICHIGAN."

"LIBERATE VIRGINIA."

And if he was on their side, they were on his—he and his supporters against some ill-defined but ever-expanding conspiracy of the Deep State that threatened their livelihoods and his presidency.

Grievance bound Trump to his supporters and them to him. It was a potent glue. Religious conservatives were aggrieved that abortion was still legal…blue collar men were aggrieved at the loss of economic power and respect…white supremacists were aggrieved at the country's changing demographics. Modernity had opened the gate to the unthinkable. Gay people could marry. Women were taking men's jobs—and becoming their bosses. Boys proclaimed themselves to actually be girls. Immigrants spilled over the border. Cops got prosecuted for killing black people. Muslims won elections to congress. When the aggrieved complained, they got labeled as bigots. All they wanted was to put everything back the way it was.

Trump spoke to them—and for them. He had entered the political arena during Obama's presidency as a super-sized personification of Grievance, capital G, the chip on his shoulder paraded proudly. With the bearing of a Mafia don, he squashed those who displeased him. Bugs on the bottom of his shoe. Trump's volcanic rage, resentment, and bigotry were proxies for people forced to grudgingly suppress what a modernizing society told them were inappropriate thoughts and feelings. Trump flaunted those feelings and got away with it. Got away with everything. And after he had verbally pummeled someone, that person, often enough, would crawl back to kiss his ring.

When elites looked down on Trump and his antics, those who shared his socially unacceptable beliefs saw a man who could put those who scorned him—and them—in their place.

If Trump was displeased, they were displeased. If he was cheated, they were cheated. Go ahead, rough up a protester, Trump had told them. He'd pay your legal bills. They loved him for it.

He told it the way it was, or how they believed it was. Yes, in the eyes of his supporters, Trump was an honest man.

And so, it might not have made much difference to some of those supporters whether votes from majority-Democratic urban centers were technically fraudulent or just cast by people they didn't see as part of "the real America." Democrats, Black Lives Matters members, antifa, and their sympathizers, were why the country wasn't great any more, and needed to be made great again. Those who wanted to move the country forward were de facto enemies. Trump's grievances and theirs, echoed back to one another, became not just reasonable but admirable. Patriotic.

The available evidence suggests that Trump understood, by the spring of 2020, that his prospects for his re-election were in jeopardy. He began specifically attacking mail-in ballots that his internal polling must have shown would increase his opponent's advantage. Several states had broadened the criteria under which voters could request mail-in ballots as a safety measure during the pandemic. A Trump tweet from May 2020 is typical of what became relentless attacks:

"There is NO WAY (ZERO!) that Mail-In Ballots will be anything less than substantially fraudulent. Mailboxes will be robbed, ballots will be forged & even illegally printed out & fraudulently signed." The reality was that several states already voted exclusively by mail, and had for years, without increases in fraud.

He broadened his attacks beyond mailed ballots, sowing doubt in the legitimacy of any outcome that didn't keep him in the White House.

"...the only way we're going to lose this election is if the election is rigged. Remember that," he proclaimed at a rally in Oshkosh, Wisconsin, in August 2020. He would repeat that allegation so often in the coming months that doubt coalesced into truth among many of his supporters. Trump couldn't lose. If the "fake media" as he called them, reported otherwise, it proved they were part of the anti-Trump conspiracy.

Independently of Trump's legal team, Sidney Powell would soon after file lawsuits in four states that repeated the rigged voting machine and

SIEGE

vast Democratic party conspiracy allegations she and Giuliani made on Fox News and at press conferences. But when official members of Trump's legal team brought court challenges on his behalf, such claims were missing from their court documents. Lawyers who file frivolous suits or openly lie to courts face consequences. (Giuliani's false claims of rigging would eventually lead New York to suspend his license, while, for her role in the fiasco, Sidney Powell would be sanctioned in federal court).

The lawyers in Trump's legal team who weren't grandstanding for the cameras didn't just omit claims of fraud, rigging, or corrupted voting machines from their complaints. In one Pennsylvania case, after Giuliani began spouting conspiracy theories during oral arguments, his co-counsel expressly stated that they were *not* claiming fraud or other misconduct.

That lawsuit asked, instead, as other legal complaints did, that millions of votes be tossed on technicalities that involved vanishingly few ballots, had nothing to do with fraud, and wouldn't have changed who won the election.

The issue in the Pennsylvania case: One voter, who had voted early in one county, wasn't allowed to fix an error he'd made on his ballot prior to election day, so his vote wasn't counted. Meanwhile, a different early voter in a second county was allowed to fix an error he'd made on his, so the second voter's ballot was counted.

The attempt to overturn a state's entire election over something so minor was certainly outrageous. But there was not a word in the complaint about hacked Dominion voting machines, or thousands of long-dead people casting ballots, or hundreds of thousands of undocumented immigrants illegally voting, or counterfeit ballots snuck into vote-counting facilities in the middle of the night—all mainstays of Giuliani's and Powell's rhetoric.

The allegations broadcast over the airwaves weren't just at odds with

10

the claims presented in court documents; they appeared to be directed at an entirely separate audience.

Trump loyalists had no reason to suspect that the judges who were tossing case after case—sixty-one out of the sixty-two filed by Trump and his allies—were hearing something different from what they were hearing broadcast on TV, expanded on social media, and amplified by rightwing personalities. If one were to accept as fact what Trump and his spokespeople alleged, it would stand to reason that any judge who refused to throw out such obviously fraudulent election results had to be part of the conspiracy.

If you were a patriotic American who consumed news and other information only from Trump-supporting media sources, social media, and conspiracy sites, it probably seemed to you that you were watching a coup in progress. And you were—just not the one you imagined.

An ad that ran in *The Washington Times* in early December 2020, and was tweeted and re-tweeted by high level Trump advisers, urged Trump to declare martial law, suspend the constitution, and have the military supervise a national re-vote. It warned that the alternative was "massive violence and destruction on a level not seen since the Civil War."

If you believed that the only two choices had been laid out for you—martial law or civil war—you might decide you had to fight, literally, with guns, bats, knives, bare hands, whatever you had, to save your country.

The United States of America was divided, not just politically, but also over what its citizens understood to be reality.

Through months of stoking vote-rigging claims, Trump never once let on that he was less than one-hundred-percent as convinced as his followers.

In a phone call with acting attorney general, Jeffrey A. Rosen, and acting deputy attorney general, Richard P. Donoghue, on December 27, 2020, Trump complained that the Department of Justice was doing a poor job of investigating rampant fraud and threatened to replace Rosen with Jeffrey Clark, a balding, bespectacled lawyer and acting head of the Justice Department's civil division whose appearance suggested more a mild-mannered accountant than a coup mastermind. Trump might have made the swap, had not the rest of the DOJ's top officials threatened to resign on the spot if he did.

Clark had, of his own volition, drafted a letter for the acting attorney general and his deputy to sign (which Rosen and Donoghue refused to do) that claimed the DOJ was investigating fraud in Georgia sufficient to change the winner in the state from Biden to Trump. This was wildly untrue, of course. The DOJ, under former Attorney General Bill Barr, who had quit just days earlier, had already announced that it had never found any such evidence. But it would have provided a fig leaf to the state's Republican officials if they decided to overturn their own election. The letter suggested that Georgia's Republican legislative leaders ignore the state's official results and instead, appoint their own slate of electors. This rogue slate would then cast the state's electoral votes for Trump.

Of course, Trump could not hang onto the presidency if just one state participated in Clark's audacious plan. Georgia had sixteen electoral votes and Trump had lost by seventy-four. Trump would need to wrest from Biden half that, plus one—at least thirty-eight electoral votes—to steal back the presidency.

But Clark hoped to persuade the Republican officials of several other states to overturn their own elections, as well. In the email in which he presented it to Rosen and Donoghue, Clark called it: "Georgia Proof of Concept." His plan was to send tailored versions of such letters to several states Biden had won but that had majority Republican legislatures: Pennsylvania (twenty electoral votes), Michigan (sixteen electoral votes), Wisconsin (ten electoral votes), and Arizona (eleven electoral votes). If just three or four went along, Trump might keep the White House.

For some odd reason, Clark included Nevada in his scheme, too. Although the state had a Republican secretary of state, it had a Democratic majority in the legislature and a Democratic governor. Though Trump loyalists had met and declared themselves the state's true electors, the state's government would never have gone along.

Like several other lawyers in the Trump universe who were searching for ways to legalize a coup d'état, some of Clark's notions appeared as delusional as they were desperate. In a separate document, he suggested that smart thermostats, controlled by China, had somehow broadcast an order to Dominion voting machines to switch Trump votes to Biden.

In a meeting with the president, Rosen and Donoghue refuted the conspiracy theories, telling Trump that they had been investigated and found to be meritless.

Donoghue cautioned the president. "Understand that the DOJ can't and won't snap its fingers and change the outcome of the election. It doesn't work that way."

"I don't expect you to do that," replied Trump. "Just say that the election was corrupt and leave the rest to me and the Republican congressmen."

Just days later, in a phone call on January 2, 2021, Trump pressured Georgia's Republican Secretary of State Brad Raffensperger to "find" enough new votes to declare Trump the state's winner.

Most bizarre of all, Trump demanded, through his chief of staff, Mark Meadows, that the Department of Justice conduct a probe into a wacky theory that satellites, controlled by subversive forces in Italy linked to the CIA, had somehow beamed down a computer hack from space which, conspiracists claimed, switched Trump ballots to Biden ballots.

If Trump knew how nonsensical all of this was, he apparently didn't care, so long as it kept him ensconced in the White House. Or maybe Trump had drunk his own Kool-Aid. Without benefit of mind-reading, it's impossible to be sure.

Whatever the case, the tainted brew got guzzled by the barrel among members of far-right groups. Social media sites lit up with comments about storming the Capitol to "stop the steal." Oath Keepers, QAnon, Three Percenters, and others organized nationwide to caravan to DC, intent on preventing congress from certifying what their president had told them were fraudulent electoral college votes.

But most of those charged with security in the US capital viewed all the social media chatter as bluster, and the upcoming rally as just the ordinary exercise of first amendment rights. DC saw protests every day. What was one more?

Even after Trump tweeted to his followers that he now had concrete proof that he'd won ("Statistically impossible to have lost the 2020 Election. Big protest in D.C. on January 6th. Be there, will be wild!"), law enforcement brass mostly yawned.

Time and again, Trump promoted the big event coming up on January 6th, admonishing supporters to fight for the future of their country. At a rally two days prior, he had this to say: "If the liberal Democrats take the Senate and the White House—and they're not taking this White House—we're going to fight like hell, I'll tell you right now. We're going to take it back."

Still, was this anything more than standard Trump bravado? The election was over. Soon, the current president would be a former president and he, even if mid-tantrum, would be shown the door.

Blindness to what was happening in plain sight was the constant—among reporters, law enforcement, government officials, and ironically enough, the insurrectionists, themselves.

The chatter among Oath Keepers, a far-right militia group with a membership heavily weighted toward former law enforcement and military personnel, was that Trump might declare martial law, and in that way, hold onto power indefinitely. Oath Keepers' founder, Stewart Rhodes, told members it was critical to be in DC on January 6th to thwart those who were attempting a coup against Trump. In their eyes, they were defenders of democracy against treacherous antifa and Black Lives Matters members. They had to be ready if Trump called upon them as a militia to help put down an insurrection.

They failed to realize that they were the ones bringing the insurrection. If their logic was muddled, none among them appeared to notice.

Not everyone was quite so oblivious. But those who saw January 6th coming were dismissed or ignored.

Congresswoman Frederica Wilson (D-FL) had firsthand experience of what could happen when Trump inflamed his supporters. In October 2017, a US Army Special Forces sergeant whom Congresswoman Wilson had known since he was a child, was among the four soldiers killed in an ambush in Niger. As Wilson accompanied the soldier's pregnant widow, his two small children, and other relatives to an airfield to accept his remains, a condolence call came in from then-President Trump. According to Wilson, Trump told the grieving wife that, although he understood it hurt, her husband "knew what he was signing up for." The young widow wept through the president's insensitive remarks, her body rolled almost into fetal position, Wilson later complained to reporters.

Trump, livid at the congresswoman's criticism, claimed he had proof she'd fabricated the account, despite several witnesses in the car confirming the accuracy of her statements.

Death threats poured in to Congresswoman Wilson's Washington, DC office.

Trump's spat with the congresswoman involved a small blow to his pride, a flea bite compared to the prospect of losing the power of the presidency. As she would later tell *19th News*, Wilson had been monitoring the violent post-election online chatter of Trump supporters and understood that the MAGA force's response was gearing up to be equal to the stakes.

On December 30, 2020, she put in a call to a female captain at the Capitol Police and had her chief-of-staff record their exchange.

As many as 50,000 people could descend on Washington, intent on keeping Trump in power, she told the captain. At minimum, their online messages signaled that they intended to march on the Capitol. Some of the chatter suggested a plan to storm the building.

What if the worst happened, and police weren't prepared? Such a pumped-up, angry mob could kill half of Congress and Vice President Mike Pence, too.

The captain didn't seem to share the congresswoman's concerns, stressing that the protesters' first amendment rights had to be honored. But she told Wilson that, if needed, there would be enough security and reinforcements.

Wilson was not assuaged.

What, exactly, did "enough" mean? she demanded to know. The whole Capitol Police force wouldn't be "enough" against such a massive mob. Were they calling up reinforcements from state and local police in neighboring jurisdictions?

The captain said no, but they could be called in "at the drop of a hat." She assured the congresswoman that such drastic measures probably wouldn't be necessary.

So—no reinforcements. Wilson grew more concerned.

What about barricades? Where were they constructing them and how high?

The captain tried again to placate Wilson. They had all the barricades they needed, she said. Three feet tall.

Exasperated by what she was hearing of the minimal preparations, Wilson replied, "Go back and tell your boss that Congresswoman Wilson said for him to get the National Guard there. Get all the surrounding jurisdiction police forces to stand around the little barricade you have."

The captain thanked the congresswoman and agreed to deliver her message to higher-ups. But Wilson could tell she was defeated.

No one was going to listen.

A day after Wilson, on December 31, 2020, Congresswoman Maxine Waters (D-CA) called Capitol Police Chief Steven Sund. She also had been a target of Trump's ire, knew that members of the Proud Boys and other potentially violent groups had already begun streaming into DC. She recognized that the situation could get ugly fast. Waters asked many of the same questions as Congresswoman Wilson had, and got the same sort of answers: don't worry. It's under control. When she inquired about the police plan, should the protesters march on the Capitol, Waters recalls that he insisted that the protesters would get nowhere near the complex.

What Wilson and Waters could not know at the time was that Capitol Police intelligence analysts had also been looking at the online chatter, and recognized that, unlike earlier pro-Trump protests, the targets weren't anti-Trump demonstrators but, as the congresswomen had inferred, lawmakers like themselves. Posts on a website called thedonald.win were particularly alarming:

"Anyone going armed needs to be mentally prepared to draw down on [law enforcement officers]. Let them shoot first, but makes sure they know what happens if they do."

"If they don't show up, we enter the Capitol as the Third

Continental Congress and certify the Trump Electors."
"Bring guns. It's now or never."
"Surround every building with a tunnel entrance/exit. They
better dig a tunnel all the way to China if they want to escape."

A special threat assessment from Capitol Police intelligence analysts
quoted about thirty such comments on the website. It was provided
to the Assistant Chief of Protective and Intelligence Operations
Yogananda D. Pittman, along with a summary that laid out the dangers:

*"Supporters of the current President see January 6, 2021, as
the last opportunity to overturn the results of the presidential
election. This sense of desperation and disappointment may lead
to more of an incentive to become violent. Unlike previous post-
election protests, the targets of the pro-Trump supporters are not
necessarily the counter-protesters as they were previously, but
**rather Congress itself is the target on the 6th. As outlined
above, there has been a worrisome call for protesters to
come to these events armed and there is the possibility that
protesters may be inclined to become violent.** [emphasis
added]*

*"...Stop the Steal's propensity to attract white supremacists, militia
members, and others who actively promote violence may lead to
a significantly dangerous situation for law enforcement and the
general public alike."*

This information apparently was never shared beyond the Capitol
Police intelligence division. Neither Police Chief Sund or others in

command staff, let alone the lower echelon officers who would actually face these dangers, saw the threat assessment. Nor was it shared with the FBI, Secret Service, National Guard, Metropolitan Police, and other law enforcement agencies during a virtual meeting on January 5, to discuss security for both January 6 and inauguration day, two weeks hence.

Instead, the Capitol Police Force's Daily Intelligence Report, issued by Pittman's office on January 4, 2021, listed the "...level of probability of acts of civil disobedience/arrests occurring based on current intelligence information" as "remote to improbable."

The report went on to note, in support of the improbability of any serious concerns, that "The Secretary of Homeland Security has not issued an elevated or imminent alert at this time."

Capitol Police brass had no way of knowing that some in the Department of Homeland Security had indeed raised alarms about the potential for significant violence by those heading to the city at Trump's command. The information just never made it into an alert.

Leadership at the Department of Homeland Security (DHS), like other agencies, had been co-opted by Trump to support his agenda.

Earlier in the year, in Portland, Oregon, DHS investigators had been instructed by the Trump loyalists at the agency to label all protesters as "violent antifa-anarchist inspired" unless proven otherwise. That mindset, if not that specific order, might have colored domestic intelligence sharing by the agency about January 6th. Trump supporters weren't supposed to be on the threat radar—not even when they were posting plans of potentially murderous attacks against legislators and the vice president on public forums.

DHS employees whose job it was to monitor online threats and send out alerts were picking up the same worrisome signs as others, and texted about them. "I feel like people are actually going to try and hurt politicians," one wrote to a colleague. Some agreed that it wouldn't be safe in Washington, DC, on January 6th, and said they would stay home that day to avoid the violence.

Perhaps confused about the orders from above that dismissed any domestic concerns that didn't involve antifa or BLM, the one thing they didn't do was the job they were hired to do: produce an official DHS threat alert.

Though the two congresswomen's entreaties failed to get traction, Capitol Police Chief Sund did reach out to the sergeants-at-arms of both the Senate and the House, asking for permission to put the National Guard on emergency stand-by. His request was rejected.

Sund would later say that he had no reason to expect Trump's January 6th Save America rally to be much different from earlier Million MAGA March Trump rallies at the Supreme Court in November and December 2020. But he was not privy to his own intelligence division's threat assessment.

Still, some rank-and-file officers among the Capitol Police had seen disturbing posts on social media and alerted higher-ups through the chain-of-command of the need for contingency planning. Their alarms, too, were ignored.

Meanwhile, local Republican parties in North Carolina, Texas, and Georgia, posted what should have been raised alarms among any viewing it: a flyer on Facebook, its headline written in a font reminiscent of that used by the Third Reich, titled "Operation Occupy the Capitol." The text used an out-of-context Abraham Lincoln quote as a battle cry to "overthrow the men who pervert the Constitution," and called for the January 6th occupation of all fifty state capitols as well as that of Washington, DC. It closed with the QAnon hashtag, #WeAreTheStorm, along with #1776Rebel and #OccupyCapitols.

The official response, predictably: no response at all.

A relatively new social media platform, Parler, that promised "free and lawful speech and expression on a viewpoint-neutral platform," was popular with Trump supporters who feared censorship on more established social media. It quickly became a hotbed of conspiracy theories and threats. The site's owners included billionaire Rebekah Mercer, a major Trump backer, and Dan Bongino, a far-right podcasting personality and former Secret Service agent, who used his platform to promote Trump's claims that the election was rigged against him. But even Parler drew the line on some messages members wrote on its website.

Beginning on December 22, 2020, Parler forwarded to the FBI those posts including specific threats of organized violence and insurrection at the Capitol planned for January 6th. On January 2, 2021, for example, Parler sent a series of posts to the agency from a user who said that armed people would be at the Capitol on January 6, 2021 and an insurrection would be necessary because "Trump needs us to cause chaos to enact the #insurrectionact."

The FBI response: no response at all.

While intelligence officials ignored a mountain of intel, Trump's acting Secretary of Defense Christopher Miller, installed in his post, in a surprise move, just days after Trump lost the 2020 election, went one better. Or worse.

Some saw the post-election firing of Miller's predecessor, Mark Esper, as an ominous event in a slow-moving self-coup attempt. But others pooh-poohed that notion, pointing out that the defense secretary is a civilian, not a member of the military, and couldn't initiate a military coup. True enough. But as the civilian head of the armed forces, the defense secretary does have significant authority. He would become, in essence, the wielder of the proverbial monkey wrench in the defense toolbox.

DC National Guard Commander William Walker had had, until January 6th, the authority to decide when, where, and how to deploy emergency Guard forces, once a decision was made to call them up.

Not this time.

In an unusual move, for the upcoming Save America rally, Miller stripped Walker of much of his authority. In January 5, 2021 memo, Miller limited the number of Guard soldiers who could be called to assist in any emergency on January 6th to three-hundred-forty. Those soldiers were not to be issued "weapons, ammunition, bayonets, batons, riot control agents or ballistic protection equipment such as helmets and body armor," without his express permission. They were also forbidden to engage in law enforcement activity, surveillance, intelligence, or have any interaction with protesters, except for self-defense.

Miller's memo ordered Walker to get the personal authorization of both the secretary of the army, Ryan McCarthy, and himself before responding to any request... or taking any action at all.

This memo was a striking departure from previous protocol. At minimum, it ensured a delay if the Guard were called upon to help contain any violence. Not in nineteen years, Walker would later testify, had he seen anything like it.

Some in law enforcement leadership were alert to the potential threat from Trump supporters on January 6th—just not the ones who would be called upon in an emergency.

The New York Police Department had been monitoring rightwing posts on social media, and determined there was a likelihood of extremist violence at the Capitol on January 6th. It sent a packet of raw intelligence on its findings to the FBI, the Capitol Police, and the Department of Homeland Security. The NYPD's expectation was that this information would be incorporated into the FBI's intelligence bulletin and the DHS's threat assessment. Neither agency would release such alerts.

A local office of the FBI in Norfolk, Virginia, distributed its own situational information report on January 5, 2021, warning of extremists traveling to DC for the Stop the Steal protests and Save America rally. Perhaps most alarming, the FBI's Norfolk office found that these militants were sharing diagrams of the tunnels beneath the Capitol.

The report, which was provided to Capitol Police intelligence, read in part:

> *"An online thread discussed specific calls for violence to include stating 'Be ready to fight. Congress needs to hear glass breaking, doors being kicked in, and blood from their BLM and Pantifa [sic] slave soldiers being spilled. Get violent. Stop calling this a march, or rally, or a protest. Go there ready for war. We get our President or we die. NOTHING else will achieve this goal.'"*

The FBI memo never made it to Police Chief Sund's desk. He would later say that he would have prepared differently if it had.

Against this backdrop, several congress members and staff noticed some peculiar activity in the Capitol on January 5, 2021, the day prior to the scheduled rally. Due to Covid-19 pandemic restrictions, public and most private tourist visits to the complex had been suspended. Yet, they reported seeing groups of visitors, decked out in red MAGA baseball caps, Trump campaign t-shirts, scarves, and similar paraphernalia, wandering the halls unescorted. Congresswoman Norma Torres (D-CA), noticed two groups of Trump supporters in the Rayburn Building, a part of the Capitol complex where congressional reps have offices, and even checking out the sub-basement, which was off-limits to tourists during normal times. Among the representatives who witnessed such unusual activity was Congresswoman Mikie Sherrill (D-NJ). It looked to the former Navy helicopter pilot and federal prosecutor like a reconnaissance trip. The tours were so far outside norms that her chief-of-staff reported the activity to the House sergeant-at-arms, asking who they were and who had allowed them in. These concerns, like the others brought to the attention of the officials charged with protection of the Capitol, failed to elicit any meaningful response.

QAnon members, the cult-like conspiracy theorists who formed part of the pro-Trump universe, were fond of saying, ominously: "The Storm is coming."

With the insurrectionists' warlike preparations, acting Defense Secretary Christopher Miller's neutering of the DC National Guard commander, and the inattentiveness of law enforcement intelligence officials, the coming rally was taking on the aspect of a perfect storm.

2

Gathering

"If POTUS allows this to occur... we're driving a stake in the heart of the federal republic."

—Text from Congressman Chip Roy (R-TX) to Trump Chief of Staff Mark Meadows

B y the day before the planned Save America rally, Washington, DC was crowded with Trump supporters who had traveled from every state, by bus, car, plane, and train. Most were unaffiliated with any particular faction. Others were organized into groups including Proud Boys, QAnon, Oath Keepers, and Three Percenters. Many, among both the organized groups and the unaffiliated Trump supporters, were believers in the hate-filled conspiracies spread by Alex Jones on InfoWars. For decades, Jones had promoted virtually every major tragedy—the Oklahoma City bombing, the 9/11 attacks, the Sandy Hook school massacre— as a staged event, or a covert government operation, or both. These "false flags," in Jones's telling, were meant to provide cover for an intrusive government intent on imposing martial law and/or as excuses to confiscate privately owned guns.

Jones had amassed wealth and power by weaving paranoid, often outlandish anti-government fantasies for popular consumption. Only now, he was on the side of the head of government, Donald J. Trump, whom he'd taken to painting as a government skeptic, much like himself, despite Trump's position as the ultimate government insider, both in the country and the rest of the world.

Jones's lieutenant, Owen Shroyer, shouting from a lectern set up on this rainy night in a park just to the east of the White House, expanded on the theme.

"I can tell you that the crooked politicians that occupy our Capitol are in fear right now. You know how I know this? Because they're scurrying around in secret tunnels to avoid 'we the people.' Right now, as we speak, they're scurrying around, like the little rats that they are, to try to avoid you. Now, why would they be doing that? Because they know they're corrupt. They know they're criminals. But worst of all, they know that *we* know."

Shroyer, on his own InfoWars show, The War Room, had once claimed that Michelle Obama was actually a transgender woman called Michael who was trying to sexualize children and take demonic culture mainstream. He and Jones both promoted the "Pizzagate" conspiracy theory, a wild fabrication accusing Democrats of running a child sex ring out of the basement of a Washington, DC, pizza parlor (which, in addition to having nothing to do with child sex trafficking, had no basement). That dark fable helped spawn later QAnon delusions. On yet another War Room episode, Shroyer called for Barack Obama's lynching.

But today, as Alex Jones's warm-up act, he mostly stayed focused on Trump's perceived enemies, and false claims that the Covid-19 pandemic was all just an elaborate Deep State ruse to keep people locked in their homes.

A rally crowd of a thousand or more, some wearing tactical gear and carrying baseball bats, or draped in flags and Trump paraphernalia, responded with chants of *"USA! USA! USA! USA!"*

They booed at the mention of Nancy Pelosi, and cheered when Shroyer proclaimed, "Trump is your daddy." They kept on cheering as he introduced Alex Jones, who yelled over the roar of the crowd:

"I don't know how all of this is going to end, but if they wanted a fight, they better believe they got one."

Though the pro-Trump swarms and their rhetoric were concerning, for DC Mayor Muriel Bowser, the administration's over-the-top response to earlier Black Lives Matter protests, both in DC, and Portland, Oregon, might have been the greater worry. In June 2020, Attorney General William Barr decided to "flood the city" with 5,800 federal troops and other personnel, including those from the National Guard, Secret Service, US Park Police, FBI, DEA, US Marshals Service, Bureau of Prisons, and other federal agencies. These forces wore no insignia to indicate their names or which agencies they were with. In July, the Trump administration cleared Portland streets with the aid of Custom and Border Protection's Border Control Unit (BORTAC), a militarized force that was reported to be intensely loyal to the president. News reports featured images of people being snatched off the streets and hustled into unmarked vans, Third World-style. Trump told Fox News at the time, "We'll go into all the cities, any of the cities" to quell unrest. He said he was prepared to send in 75,000 federal officers. Meanwhile, Barr made noises about seizing control of the Washington, DC, Metropolitan Police Force (MPD).

Mayor Bowser requested only a small force of unarmed National Guard troops to assist with traffic and similar duties, in order to free up MPD officers for protest-related calls. To pre-empt the possibility of greater federal involvement—and overreach—during the coming rallies, Bowser sent a letter to acting Defense Secretary Christopher Miller, acting Attorney General Jeffrey Rosen, and Army Secretary Ryan McCarthy, telling them that DC didn't need or want federal troops deployed for the January 6th rallies; she tweeted the relevant section:

"To be clear, the District of Columbia is not requesting other federal law enforcement personnel and discourages any additional deployment without immediate notification to, and consultation with, MPD if such plans are underway."

Congresswoman Zoe Lofgren (D-CA), chair of the House committee responsible for Capitol Police oversight, and Congressman Tim Ryan (D-OH), chair of the House committee with financial oversight of the force, each held separate conference calls with Capitol Police Chief Sund. He assured them that all necessary precautions were in place for the next day's events. In telling Lofgren that the National Guard would be on standby, he failed to mention that his request for calling in National Guard back-up had been denied.

Meanwhile, as many as two dozen Trump allies, including Steve Bannon, Rudy Giuliani, Roger Stone, and Trump's two eldest sons, Donald Jr., and Eric, gathered in so-called war rooms in two Washington, DC, hotels, to finalize their January 6th strategy.

As night falls, and tens of thousands attend rallies and speeches, and make plans for the big events the following day, one individual walks the streets of DC alone. Caught for seconds at a time at one or another of the ubiquitous security cameras posted by homeowners, businesses, and government agencies around the city, the person appears, at first, to be lost, or maybe looking for something or someone.

Of short to medium stature, it's unclear whether this is a man or woman, so let's call the person "they." They wear a light gray hoodie, pulled so close around the face, it hides any features that might not already be obscured behind the surgical mask that they, like most others, wear to avoid catching or spreading Covid-19. Their other apparel is mostly generic: dark loose-fitting pants, dark gloves. Only the black and gray sneakers are distinctive: Nike Air Max Speed Turfs. The person carries a medium gray backpack in one hand.

The backpack appears to be weighty. Resting it for a moment against the stone retaining wall of a residential block on South Capitol Street at about 7:40 pm, the person adjusts the glasses on their face, stands on tiptoes to peer at something or someone on the other side of the street, then hides their face behind a gloved hand as a man, walking a dog, passes by. The person then quickly walks back in the direction they came.

Something about the body language and what little of the body shape can be discerned under the clothing suggests youth, possibly femininity, possibly both. Or perhaps this impression is just due to stature.

About twelve minutes later, another camera catches the person stopping to rest on a park bench near the Democratic National Committee headquarters.

After adjusting clothing worn under each of the sleeves of the hoodie jacket—bra straps that had drifted down over the upper arms?—the person slumps to fish around in the pack while checking their surroundings.

Caught again on video twenty-two minutes later, they walk purposefully down an alley between the Capitol Hill Club and the Republican National Committee headquarters, next appearing

in front of the Capitol Hill Club, where they stretch their arms
above and behind them in a classic gesture of released tension.
The backpack is, by now, far less weighty.

January 6, 2021

Early that morning, as he drove to work, Police Chief Sund called DC Metropolitan Police Inspector Robert Glover, to get his sense of the crowds converging about two miles away from the Capitol on the Ellipse, the large oval field just south of the White House where Trump was scheduled to speak in a few hours. The MPD had primary jurisdiction over the city outside federal buildings and property. Glover told Sund the crowd was large but orderly, lining up early to get into the event. So far, so good, but there had been clashes between Trump supporters and counter-protesters during the Million MAGA Marches in November and December.

Chief Sund had what he thought was a good plan, should the rally-goers become unruly. All sworn officers would be working except who'd been on duty the previous night. About half the officers would have "hard gear" available, if needed: helmets, shields, and protective clothing.

The day prior, at Senate Sergeant-at-Arms Stenger's suggestion, he'd called the DC National Guard's Commander, General Walker, to ask how many National Guard the general could provide and how quickly he could provide them, should they be needed, and assuming Sund got approval to make the request, which, as yet, he hadn't. General Walker assured him that 125 of the National Guard could be called upon to assist quickly. Believing he'd prepared as much as necessary, he entered the Capitol Police Command Center, where a bank of monitors displayed live video from key points around the capital city and the

Capitol, itself. Flanked by aides and assistant chiefs, Sund took his seat at the center console and requested a feed of the activity at the National Mall and Ellipse.

Over on the Ellipse stage, Congressman Mo Brooks (R-AL), the first speaker at the Save America rally, was riling up the audience;

> *"... today, Republican senators and congressmen have a simple choice. Today, Republican senators and congressmen will either vote to turn America into a godless, amoral, dictatorial, oppressed and socialist nation on the decline, or they will join us or they will fight and vote against voter fraud and election theft and vote for keeping America great."*

The rhetoric, though extreme, was in keeping with what team Trump had been spouting since the election.

By 9:45 am, reports told Sund that the crowds at the Ellipse were expected to exceed their permitted attendee numbers of thirty-thousand.

Congresswoman Susan Ellis Wild (D-PA), along with her Democratic congressional colleagues Madeleine Dean, Mary Gay Scanlon, and Chrissy Houlahan, had swept into Congress in 2019, as part of what had been, until then, an all-male Pennsylvania delegation. Local media had nicknamed them the "Fab Four," for bringing the strength of women's voices in representing the state.

Wild had started that morning feeling annoyed, and more willing than was her usual style to express that annoyance. Eight members of Pennsylvania's Republican delegation planned to object to the certification of the state's electoral votes, for no discernable reason other than that Donald Trump wanted them to. The objections were ludicrous, in Wild's view. Republicans, comfortably in the majority in the Pennsylvania state legislature, had loosened the rules for voting in the state's elections in 2019. Among other reforms in what was essentially a Republican initiative, they added no-excuse mail-in voting as early as fifty days before an election. Now, Trump and his allies were claiming that fraud had exploded as a result of those mail-in ballots, because the presidential election hadn't gone their way.

To Wild's thinking, that was unreasonable, illogical, and plain silly.

But fealty to—or fear of— the president was known to make some otherwise sensible people do and say things that defied logic. If Donald J. Trump claimed that little green men had dropped in from Mars to illegally cast ballots, who would be shocked if a fair number of the GOP's more ambitious politicians searched the skies for UFOs, shooting down half the drones Best Buy had sold over Christmas?

Wild was heartened that at least one Pennsylvania Republican colleague, with whom she had worked well in the past, was not joining in this nonsense.

Having just been sworn in for her second term as the representative for Pennsylvania's seventh district, Wild joined the state's Democratic delegation for a 9:00 am Zoom meeting. For two hours, they discussed the issues likely to be raised by the objectors to Pennsylvania's vote certification. They then divided up the tasks among them of responding to each challenge.

Although the objections and responses would be time consuming, the delay couldn't change the fact that at the end of the process, Joe Biden's win would be official. And Susan Wild would have a played roles both in sweeping aside the frivolous objections and certifying his electoral college win. It didn't get much more exciting than that. Her mood lighter now, Wild prepared for what she knew would be a long day. Dressed in a dazzling red power blazer and comfortable black flats, she packed a phone charger, some sliced Gouda, and bottled water in a backpack, and set out at about 11:00 am to participate in history.

Congresswoman Wild wasn't the first member of her family to enter politics. Her son, Clay Wild, 27, had made it to Washington, DC, years before his mom, in 2013, when he became an intern in the Obama White House.

Moving up to a staff position as a writer in June 2014, he was part of a team that drafted many of the words that Obama spoke and "wrote" during his tenure. And when Obama left office, Clay joined his post-presidency team for six months.

Now, Clay Wild was embarking on a new career. After graduating law school in May 2020, and joining a Washington, DC, law firm, he'd gotten word, just weeks before, that he'd passed the bar.

January 6th found the newly minted lawyer in North Carolina, taking a much needed break. As was his morning habit, he turned on the TV news, more as background noise than as the focus of his attention. He vaguely noticed something about a big Trump rally, but protests were a common occurrence in DC, and if Trump's overheated rhetoric drew angry throngs in MAGA gear to his event, well, what else was new? Clay had learned to mostly ignore protests, although, granted, such gatherings had become more raucous and even aggressive since his time working in the Obama White House.

Mostly, he was relieved that the Trump era was ending. When Trump first rode down that golden escalator in 2015 to announce his candidacy, Clay, like virtually everyone he knew, treated it as a joke, a stunt. The reality show mogul hadn't even had any actual supporters on hand for his presidential bid announcement, so he'd had to put out a casting call, and pay people fifty bucks each to wave signs and cheer him on.

How things had changed.

Still, Clay took it for granted that, despite a post-election, sore-loser-driven, giant clown show's worth of challenges, the Trump regime was done, and the United States of America would have a peaceful, orderly transition to the next administration. As always.

But Trump was far from finished fighting the notion of a transition, peaceful or otherwise. Grasping for any means to hang onto power, his latest refrain was that Vice President Mike Pence could and should refuse to certify the electoral college votes of certain states that Biden had won. And by refusing to certify, Pence would give Trump an eleventh hour chance at a second term. Better than just a chance: a certainty.

In reality, Pence had no authority to do anything but preside over the counting of the electoral votes already certified by the states. But a bizarre and radical notion that the vice president had the right to singlehandedly overturn a presidential election had taken hold in Trumpist circles.

That morning, at 8:17, Trump had tweeted:

"All Mike Pence has to do is send them back to the States, AND WE WIN. Do it Mike, this is a time for extreme courage!"

Soon, on the Ellipse stage, Rudy Giuliani, among the warm-up speakers for the president on this chilly morning, would repeat the demand that Pence refuse to accept the ballots.

"[Pence] can decide on the validity of these crooked ballots, or he can send it back to the legislators, give them five to ten days to

34

finally finish the work. We now have letters from five legislators begging us to do that. They're asking us. Georgia, Pennsylvania, Arizona, Wisconsin, and one other coming in.

"It seems to me, we don't want to find out, three weeks from now, even more proof that this election was stolen, do we?

"Over the next ten days, we get to see the machines that are crooked, the ballots that are fraudulent, and if we're wrong, we will be made fools of. But if we're right, a lot of them will go to jail.

"Let's have trial by combat. I'm willing to stake my reputation, the president is willing to stake his reputation, on the fact that we're going to find criminality there."

After months of making outrageous claims in court and elsewhere, Giuliani didn't have much of a reputation left to stake. But "trial by combat"— hand-to-hand battle, Game of Thrones-style, to determine a winner—apparently sounded good to the ever-swelling crowd whose members cheered him on with chants of "*Rudy, Rudy, Rudy.*"

Unlike Clay Wild, Florida Democratic Congresswoman Frederica Wilson was not convinced that this presidential transition would be peaceful, if it happened at all. She'd had no luck persuading the Capitol Police captain she'd spoken to the week before that they needed to institute far greater precautions than planned. And now, she was terrified of what awaited as she traveled to the Capitol to cast a vote.

She had her driver take her early, arriving at 10:30. Although Trump's Save America rally was taking place almost two miles away, what she estimated to be hundreds of Trump supporters were gathered near the Capitol. The perimeter of the complex was supposed to be surrounded by fencing, but a closer look belied that label. The "fencing" was nothing more than green plastic garden netting, designed to keep rabbits and deer away from plantings.

Maybe, to some, the scores of middle-aged white people dressed in silly outfits topped with MAGA hats looked about as threatening as rabbits—perhaps less disconcerting to a majority white officialdom than the sea of black faces that had last summer shown up to demonstrate against the murder of George Floyd by a Minneapolis police officer. But after Wilson's spat with Trump in 2017 stirred up hate against her, she knew, appearances aside, what some of the more avid Trump supporters were capable of. She'd also read a number of violent social media posts regarding the election. When they wrote of thwarting the electoral college ballot certification, and doing grave harm to members of Congress and the vice president, she took them at their word.

Just the merest sprinkling of police officers stood between the protesters and the building. She didn't know the protesters' intentions, but she realized immediately that those few officers wouldn't be able to stop them if those intentions were anything but benign.

Determined to get far from the Capitol, she left immediately after voting, exiting the building about 11:00 am Already, the crowd looked to have about doubled in the area near where her driver had dropped her off.

As she waited for her driver, Congresswoman Wilson saw only one police officer nearby; and he was not close enough to help, if she needed it.

The protesters might not have known exactly who she was, but as a black congresswoman, she figured they would surmise that she wasn't Trump's friend. As she made her way toward the car, she felt hundreds of eyes on her, appraising her, and not liking what they saw. No one tried to talk to her, but she sensed menace as men and women in the crowd drifted closer.

Seeing her approach, her driver put the car in gear and headed her way. Wilson rushed to the vehicle, unable to breathe easily again until the door was shut behind her.

Nothing had happened. And probably, nothing would have, at least, not at that moment. But she was taking no further chances. She didn't need to be present for the ceremonial counting of the electoral votes. She would watch, instead, on TV, from the safety of her apartment, several blocks away.

Police reports had, by now, noted crowds forming at a number of locations around the building's perimeter. Among them were about two-hundred Proud Boys, the male-only neo-fascist organization of self-described "western chauvinists" known for street fighting, for racist, homophobic, and misogynist rhetoric—and, of course, loyalty to Trump. At a presidential debate between Trump and Biden on September 29, 2020, Fox News moderator Chris Wallace had asked Trump if he would condemn white supremacist and militia groups and tell them to stand down and not contribute to violence. Insisting that all the violence came from the left wing, Trump refused to criticize such groups, saying instead, "Proud Boys: stand back and stand by."

Taking Trump's response as a message of encouragement, by the following day, on the Telegram instant messaging service, more than five-thousand Proud Boys and their supporters would adopt the words "Stand Back," placing them above the group's logo, with "Stand By" beneath it.

Congresswoman Alexandria Ocasio-Cortez (D-NY), a frequent target of right-wing media pundits, also sensed that the Trump supporters descending on DC for the past several days had more in mind than just an exercise of their first amendment rights. She had gotten texts from other members of Congress, telling her just that: that they had heard rumblings about planned violence from people who were hard-core Trump supporters. Their advice: lay low. Something bad was coming on the 6th. And, if she wasn't on guard, that bad something would be coming for her.

Fiercely smart, and as outspoken and frank as you'd expect a New York woman to be, AOC, as she's affectionately dubbed, was the youngest congresswoman ever when first elected to Congress in 2018 at the tender age of 29. After her re-election in 2020, she was still the youngest of the current Congress. And, as an author of the environmental legislation known as The Green New Deal, a sweeping proposal that had incited the wrath of conservatives, she got more attention (much of it unwelcome) than some congress members who had been in DC for decades.

Most hardcore Trump supporters considered her the enemy. She shrugged it off. But as she returned to her electric car, parked in the Capitol lot while she cast a vote, two days before Congress was to certify the electoral college votes, she was confronted by a crowd in MAGA hats, loitering in wait, just a couple of feet away from her vehicle. Some began to yell abuse, asking her why she hated the country. Putting on a brave smile, she decided to engage them. "I love this country," she replied. "Why do you think I dedicate my life to it?"

The taunts continued as she pulled away. Shaken after that confrontation and a couple of other incidents with those pouring into the capital city to protest the electoral college ballot certification, she felt the invisible target on her back.

Her office, across the street from the Capitol, itself, was in the Cannon building, one of three buildings, including the Rayburn and Longworth buildings, where House legislators worked while not in the iconic domed structure to debate legislation and cast votes. She carpooled on the morning of January 6th with her friend and fellow "Squad" member Ayanna Pressley (D-MA), arriving about 9:30 am For safety's sake, she planned to stay away from the Capitol itself until it was time to vote.

Trump was scheduled to speak at 11:00 am, but he didn't begin until almost an hour later. Meanwhile, a short video played that, in theme and even in some images, was vaguely reminiscent of Leni Riefenstahl's much longer 1935 propaganda film of a Nazi rally, *Triumph of the Will*, that exulted Hitler as the rescuer of Germany from the forces attempting to undermine it. The Trump video, a mere two minutes long, began with an extreme close-up of the president's face completely filling the Jumbotron screen. Then, President-elect Joe Biden's, Senator Chuck Schumer's, and Congresswoman Nancy Pelosi's images appeared, accompanied by sad music. An excerpt from Trump's 2017 inauguration speech played, in which he accused a "small group in our nation's capital" of profiting "while the people have borne the costs." To punctuate the point, the film quickly cut to a number of images, meant to tie the Democrats to the ills faced by ordinary Americans —a flag-draped coffin, a man hanging his head in despair, a homeless camp—followed by Trump proclaiming: "That all changes, starting right here and right now."

Upbeat music swept away the melancholy tune. Scenes from earlier rallies replaced the somber clips. A woman wept for joy. A man tore a photo of Nancy Pelosi in half. Trump, in silhouette, appeared almost to walk on clouds. Fighter jets, more adoring crowds, signs proclaiming *"Jobs, Jobs, Jobs,"* and lastly, Big Brother-like, Trump's face again completely filled the screen.

For believers, it was an effective pay off of the theme of the rally: (only Trump can) Save America.

But he needed their help to do it.

By the time the president himself began to speak at 11:57 am, tens of thousands who had heeded his call to come to Washington, DC, on January 6th to "stop the steal" were more than ready for their mission.

He laid it out for them, in lie after lie that sounded to his supporters like biblical truth:

"This year, using the pretext of the China virus and the scam of mail-in ballots, Democrats attempted the most brazen and outrageous election theft. And there's never been anything like this. It's a pure theft in American history. Everybody knows it. That election, our election was over at ten in the evening. We're leading Pennsylvania, Michigan, Georgia by hundreds of thousands of votes. And then, late in the evening or early in the morning, boom! These explosions of bullshit, and all of the sudden — all of a sudden, it started to happen."

The crowd roared back the claim:

"Bullshit. Bullshit. Bullshit."

They were ready to go, long before he mentioned the Capitol. And then, at last, about an hour into his speech, he did.

"We're going to walk down to the Capitol and we're going to cheer on our brave senators and congressmen and women. And we're probably not going to be cheering so much for some of them. Because you'll never take back our country with weakness. You have to show strength and you have to be strong."

"Storm the Capitol," shouted voices in the crowd.

"Fight for Trump. Fight, fight, fight. Take the Capitol. Take the Capitol. Take the Capitol right now."

Proud Boys' organizers had made their plans online, often in encrypted messages using the Telegram app, where they openly mused about storming the Capitol on January 6th. Then, two days before the big rally, their leader, Enrique Tarrio, was arrested for destruction of property related to his burning of a Black Lives Matter banner the month previous. Weapons charges were added when he was discovered to be carrying high ammunition magazines that are banned in Washington, DC.

A Proud Boys' lieutenant took charge of communications and instructed other Proud Boys that their encrypted messages might now be in the hands of the police. Fearing that they could be brought up on gang charges, he stressed that there had been and would be no planning at all. But this denial appeared to be meant for authorities more than for members. Too much had already been written about plans, tactics, and strategies to cover their tracks completely, including messages to Oath Keepers members.

Agreeing to meet at the Washington Monument at 10:00 am, hundreds of Proud Boys had marched as a group to the east side of the Capitol building. Most were easy to identify by their orange knit hats and orange armbands. But leaders of the group had announced on the Parler social network that many would be attending the rally "incognito" and would perhaps even wear the all-black costumes favored by their arch-enemies, antifa. Florida Proud Boy organizer Joseph Biggs and Seattle-based lieutenant Ethan Nordean, known as "Rufio Panman," picked up where Tarrio had left off. Biggs, a burly sort, and a former writer for InfoWars, sent a message to the other sixty or so Proud Boys on the encrypted channel, about "going over tomorrow's plan." In Tarrio's absence, Nordean was in charge. Biggs wrote that he was "with Rufio," using Nordean's nom de guerre.

Proud Boys typically wore black and yellow polo shirts, but many also favored a t-shirt, sold as Proud Boy merchandise, with the slogan "Pinochet did nothing wrong," referring to the Chilean fascist dictator who was known for tossing his enemies to their death from helicopters. On the back, in case anyone didn't get the reference, was a cartoonish graphic of people being thrown out of a chopper.

Circling around to the west side of the building, they re-grouped near the Peace Monument that stands in the roundabout where Pennsylvania Avenue feeds into the Capitol grounds. Here, they merged with what officials called "a wall of people"—an enormous contingent of Trump supporters who had marched down Pennsylvania Avenue before Trump was finished speaking.

While this was happening, at 12:47 pm, Capitol Police were alerted to a suspicious device, outside the Republican National Committee headquarters, just blocks from the Capitol. They discovered a fully operational bomb, made from threaded galvanized pipe, kitchen timers, and homemade powder.

FBI officials would later determine that the bomb and one other, found at 1:15 pm near Democratic National Committee headquarters, had been planted by that mystery person, face obscured by a light gray hoodie, who carried their heavy backpack up, down, and around the streets near the Capitol the night before. As of this writing, the person's identity is still unknown.

With those discoveries, no one could be certain how many more improvised explosive devices might be planted around the city, ready to go off on this already turbulent day.

During a sweep of the area with bomb-sniffing dogs, police discovered a vehicle loaded with eleven Molotov cocktails filled with home-made napalm, as well as guns, and spare magazines. Though the FBI would later clear the vehicle's owner, Lonnie Leroy Coffman, 71, of Alabama, of planting the pipe bombs, each discovery layered chaos on top of chaos.

Officers from the Capitol Police force, already stretched as thinly as possible, got pulled away from guarding the Capitol building and grounds for the bomb investigation and to evacuate congress members and staff from the Cannon building, the legislative office building closest to the Republican National Committee headquarters, and another building between Cannon and where the first bomb was found.

Despite the MAGA crowds in the street outside, Congresswoman Ocasio-Cortez had been having a good day. Against all odds, in the two Georgia senate runoffs, both Democrats had won. Reverend Raphael Warnock had been declared the winner of the first contest early that morning and Jon Ossoff was all but certain to be declared the winner of the second at any moment. The Senate, although evenly divided at fifty/fifty, would be under Democratic control because newly elected Vice President Kamala Harris would be able to cast a vote to break any ties.

Alone in her office with just her legislative aide—the other members of her staff were working remotely due to the pandemic—AOC decided to order a celebratory lunch for herself and the aide. Completely unaware that an explosive device had just been discovered at the Republican National Committee headquarters a block and a half away, she spent about fifteen minutes on a call with her chief of staff, then started scrolling on her phone to decide from which restaurant to order a scrumptious lunch.

Suddenly, she heard violent banging on the doors in the hallway. It sounded like someone trying to break the doors down. There were no other sounds—no voices—just the banging.

Still oblivious to the bomb discoveries, all she could think was that the Trump supporters had broken into the building. And they were coming for her.

Rushing to her legislative aide's office, he yelled at her to: "Hide. *Hide!* Run and hide."

At the back of her office were two doors, one to a closet and the other to a bathroom. She rushed to the bathroom, then realized that that would be the first place they'd look. She should have hidden in the closet. But it was too late.

A booming voice came from the other side of her office door. "Where is she? Where *is* she?"

Convinced that this was the end, she lost all sense of time as she peaked through the gap where hinges attached the door to its frame. Standing on the other side was a white man in a black beanie. Terrified, she found herself slowly sliding down toward the floor until she heard the voice of her aide.

"It's okay," he called out. The man in the beanie, her aide told her, was with the Capitol Police.

Heart hammering, she listened as a seemingly very angry officer yelled at her and the aide. They had to immediately evacuate to the Longworth building through the tunnel system beneath the buildings, he said. He didn't explain why. He was probably already stressed to the max and probably assumed they knew.

Ocasio-Cortez and her aide came to the only conclusion that made sense to them, based on the information they had. The MAGA crowds must have broken through the doors, overwhelmed the police, and were in the Cannon building with them right then, hunting for those they considered their enemies.

Grabbing her bag, AOC and her aide did as they were instructed and raced from the office. Only after they came out of the tunnel into the other structure did they realize that they had no idea where they were supposed to go from there.

Around the corner, between the National Mall and the western front of the Capitol grounds, members of the MAGA mob erected a gallows. A sign at its bottom declared "THIS IS ART," but some gathered around it, including David Nicholas Dempsey of California, insisted that it should be taken more literally. Wearing a flag gaiter that obscured the bottom of his face, and goggles and helmet above, he apparently believed he was safe from being identified as he responded to questions from a person taking video.

"This isn't just art. This is necessary," opined Dempsey. The

Californian had been in and out of prison since 2006, most often on burglary charges. But the most recent charges against him were for spraying bear repellant at anti-Trump demonstrators in Santa Monica in October 2020.

"Them worthless fucking shitholes like fucking Jerry Nadler and fucking Pelosi, uh, Clapper, Comey, fucking all those pieces of garbage, you know, Obama, all these dudes, Clinton, fuck all these pieces of shit," Dempsey continued, gesturing toward the gallows. "That's what they need. They don't need a jail cell. They need to hang from these motherfuckers where everybody videotapes it and fucking spreads it on YouTube or fucking whatever other social media there is. And they need to get the point across that the time for peace talk is over."

Not far away, at entrance to the northwest side of the Capitol grounds, other Trump supporters milled around the Peace Monument. Shouting into a black bullhorn, next to Proud Boys' organizer Joe Biggs, Paul Russell Johnson, slim, bearded, from Lanexa, Virginia, led them in an increasingly hostile chant of *"USA. USA. USA. USA."*—more war cry than patriotic cheer.

Some Proud Boys wore body armor, carried baseball bats and other objects capable of being used as bludgeons, and communicated back and forth via two-way radio. Others in the crowd waved large flags on long wooden poles, emblazoned with pro-Trump slogans, or Trump's name. It was impossible to guess how many weapons were secreted in pockets and backpacks: knives, sticks, metal rods, bear spray.

Amid the growing crowd was a 37-year old Pennsylvania man named Ryan Samsel. Samsel had an ugly history of violence, most often against women. In 2011, he had beaten a pregnant girlfriend, choked her, and held her head under water. In 2015, he choked another woman to the point of unconsciousness. In 2019, yet another woman alleged that he had broken into her home, choked her and repeatedly raped her.

At about the time that Capitol Police began evacuating the Cannon building, Samsel, on parole for one offense and with a warrant out for him on another, sauntered over to chat with Joe Biggs.

All that stood between the pro-Trump mob and the five officers on the front lines were two rows of bike racks, meant to be barricades, with plastic mesh fencing covering the racks and signs stating, in red letters, "AREA CLOSED."

One of those five officers was a petite Caroline Edwards, 31, her blonde hair tied neatly under her cap. Edwards' husband was also a member of the force, but stationed elsewhere at the Capitol.

Behind Edwards and her fellow officers was a short stretch of concrete steps, and maybe a couple dozen more officers, spread across acres of lawn.

The cops were all in their patrol uniforms—no armor or protective gear of any kind. The crowd on the other side already numbered at least a thousand. And more kept coming.

Samsel's body language suggested a fighter ready for a scuffle. He left behind the Trump flag he'd been carrying and marched cockily up to the first set of barricades, knocking them over. Others from the mob fell in behind him, with Johnson using the bullhorn to taunt the cops.

"Fuck this shit. We pay your bills. You back the fuck off."

The officers stood their ground. Their best hope was that this belligerent crowd would be intimidated enough by the presence of uniformed authority to stay on the other side of the bike racks. But they kept coming, now almost nose-to-nose.

Samsel and Johnson stood for a moment, staring the officers down, then Samsel grabbed the barricade and shook it. Pulling off his denim jacket, he turned the cap of his MAGA hat backwards on his head. Taking this as a signal, Johnson and others in the mob surged forward, yanking the racks up off the ground, using them to shove the officers back several feet.

Edwards fell, her head striking the concrete steps behind her. Dazed and disoriented, she found herself pulled up from the ground by Samsel, whose words echoed in her mind as he barreled past.

"We don't have to hurt you. Why are you standing in our way?"

Clinging to a railing for support, Edwards cried for help through her radio. Officers who had been scattered across the expansive lawn raced toward the downed barricade, frantically trying to hold back the mob. It was futile. There were too few of them against too many insurgents.

At almost the same moment, shouting and whooping, on the east side of the Capitol building, another group pushed forward through bike barricades, muscling their way past a slightly larger, but still outnumbered, contingent of Capitol Police.

The siege had begun.

3

Breach

"We're taking our House back. We're not going to take your fucking vaccine.
We're not going to take your bullshit. The people are rising up!"

— Insurrectionist storming the Capitol

T he downing of the first barricade was like a bugler's call to battle. Hordes of people, many in Trump gear, trampled en masse past the meager police defenses at multiple locations around the Capitol grounds perimeter. The mob transformed the ladder-like bike rack barricades that were meant to keep them out into weapons, heaving the makeshift fences against the cops, toppling them like dominoes as they surged across the grounds.

Among those in the clash, not far behind Samsel, was Proud Boy Dominic Pezzola, 42, known as Spaz. A US Marine veteran and former boxer from Rochester, New York, Pezzola's most prominent feature was a broad nose that looked like it might have been broken a time or two. His wild salt-and-pepper hair, worn on the long side, scraggly beard, and confrontational manner suggested the quintessential street brawler. High school friends remembered him as a macho type, but some expressed shock that his political rhetoric had grown increasingly extreme in recent years.

Pezzola had at one time been a registered Democrat, switched to Independent, and now was all Trump, all the way. He'd been collecting documents on making home-made explosive and poisons—suggesting that peaceful protest wasn't necessarily in his plans.

As he joined the fierce melee, tussling with Capitol cops near the steps to the building, Pezzola wrested a police riot shield from one of the officers, then withdrew into the crowd.

He'd soon be back.

Capitol Police Chief Sund had been monitoring Trump's speech but got called away to handle the bomb threats. As Sund returned to the command center, and discovered what his officers were facing from the rioters, he immediately suspected that the bombs had been placed as diversions, meant to pull command personnel and officers away from the Capitol perimeter to allow the insurgents an opening.

Rioters had come prepared for battle, wearing helmets, gas masks, and shields. Some were coordinating with each other via earpieces and radio. Their chants grew more menacing.

> *"Whose House? Our House. Whose House? Our House."*
> *"USA! USA! USA!"*
> *"Let's get their guns."*
> *"Let's get their guuuunnns!"*

They attacked the cops with pipes, bats, pepper spray, and flag poles. Sund had never seen anything like it in his thirty years in law enforcement in Washington, DC.

He immediately called his counterpart in the Metropolitan Police Department, acting Chief of Police Robert J. Contee III, to request reinforcements. Days before, Contee had agreed to have officers from the MPD step in if needed.

Meanwhile, Major General Walker, commander of the DC Guard, got ready to pull all his forces from traffic support in the city to redeploy to the Capitol. To get ahead of the impending crisis while he awaited authorization, Walker sent a National Guard lieutenant colonel to the Capitol at the same time Contee sent the MPD. There, the lieutenant colonel met up with an MPD Deputy Chief, who wanted to know: why aren't the National Guard here already?

The lieutenant colonel was sure they were coming, he said. He had been sent "to scout out where they're going to be when they get here."

Walker's plan was to get every single guardsman to the building without delay. But his hands were tied until authorization for the re-deployment came through.

By 1:13 pm, the first contingent of MPD officers, under MPD Commander Robert Glover, arrived at the Capitol. About a hundred officers in hard riot gear, yellow and black reflective jackets, and white helmets, streamed down the steps of one of the west entrances to the building, near the scaffolding that had been erected for the presidential inaugural stage.

The officers formed a line and quickly pushed back insurrectionists from the west terrace steps. Rioters fought them with fists, sticks, pipes, and pepper spray. Glover almost immediately radioed for back-up against the mob that swelled larger by the moment. "CDU 12 up to help maintain the lines," cried Glover, asking for a civil disturbance unit. "They're throwing bike racks."

The MPD tried forcing them back with stinger ball grenades. Like flashbangs, stinger balls explode on impact, with a firecracker-like snap, a bright flare, and a puff of smoke. But unlike flashbangs, which are meant simply to disorient, when stinger balls explode, they send small rubber bullet-like pellets flying in all directions. Considered less-lethal weapons, had been used the previous June to scare off mostly peaceful Black Lives Matter demonstrators in Lafayette Square, to make way for Trump's Bible-in-hand photo op in front of a church. There, they helped break up the protest in moments. Here, though the stinger balls elicited surprised shouts of defiance and fear, their launch appeared to embolden the rioters.

"Cruiser 50," Glover identified himself to the JOC. "First sting ball deployed. No effect. Took metal debris in return."

While Capitol and Metropolitan police forces did battle with insurrectionists, Sund again pleaded with Sergeants-at-Arms Stenger and Irving to call in the National Guard. Now. Anticipating approval, and not wanting another moment's delay in pushing back the rioters before they could breach the building itself, Sund followed up with Major General Walker. His voice cracking with emotion, he called the emergency dire.

Walker assured him he could have one-hundred-fifty Guard there within twenty minutes. But he needed the request from the Capitol officials, and then approval from up the chain of command. As soon as their call ended, Walker relayed the urgency of the police chief's request to Army leaders.

A moment before Contee's MPD reinforcements arrived at the Capitol, Trump wound up his speech on the Ellipse with literal marching orders to his followers:

"We're going to walk down Pennsylvania Avenue—I love Pennsylvania Avenue— and we're going to the Capitol and we're going to

try and give... The Democrats are hopeless. They're never voting for anything, not even one vote. But we're going to try and give our Republicans, the weak ones, because the strong ones don't need any of our help, we're going to try and give them the kind of pride and boldness that they need to take back our country."

At Trump's command, they set out down Pennsylvania Avenue for the Capitol, eventually swelling the mob on the grounds to ten thousand.

Real estate agent Ryan Nichols of Longview, Texas, was the kind of guy who would drive across the country to help if he believed he was needed. In 2018, the former Marine made the trek to North Carolina to rescue victims of Hurricane Florence. And then, he went back into the storm to save the lives of six dogs left behind in a rapidly flooding kennel. Talk show host Ellen DeGeneres was so moved by his story, she invited him on her show and presented him with a check for twenty-five thousand dollars to donate to the Humane Society.

But a lot can change in two years. Wearing a camo hat, body armor, an American flag gaiter that he could pull up as a face covering, and carrying a crowbar, Nichols looked very different from the man Ellen DeGeneres had honored as an American hero. Now, he imagined himself an American revolutionary. As he marched to the Capitol with another veteran, Alex Harkrider, he live-streamed a tirade about his plans for those counting the electoral college ballots who "treasoned the country," as he put it.

"I'm telling you, if Pence caved, we're gonna drag motherfuckers through the streets. You fucking politicians are going to get fucking drug through the streets. Because we're not going to have our fucking shit stolen." Anticipating the storming of the Capitol as the second revolution, he chanted as he marched:

"Lock and load. Lock and load. Lock and load."

Scott Kevin Fairlamb, bald, wearing a brown camouflage jacket, a long scruffy lumberjack-style beard, an impassioned visage, and carrying a collapsible baton, stood ready to carry out what he perceived as the orders of his commander-in-chief. "What patriots do? We fuckin' disarm them and then we fuckin' storm the Capitol," hollered Fairlamb from the Capitol steps.

A New Jersey gym owner, angered by pandemic restrictions that closed his business, and a former mixed martial arts fighter whose stage name was Wildman, Fairlamb, 43, like many others on the Capitol steps that day, had ties to law enforcement. His brother, a Secret Service agent, had guarded Michelle Obama while she was First Lady. His father was a New Jersey state trooper. Yet, Fairlamb apparently believed, if duty to his president demanded that he beat the brother-in-blue who stood in his way, so be it. Grabbing an officer from behind, the ex-MMA fighter shoved, punched, and overpowered the cop as a police bodycam recorded the attack.

Rioters had, by this time, forced back the Capitol Police into the building and their Metropolitan Police reinforcements to just outside, allowing the mob to advance further. Some, literally, climbed the walls. Dangling from crevices in the edifice like a band of crazed macaques, they clambered blindly up where adrenaline led them.

Frenzied, jubilant, enraged, ecstatic, bloodthirsty—any and all fit the mood of these people invading their own government.

And yet, they imagined themselves patriots.

The flags of the insurrection, whipping in the chill January wind, broadcast the cognitive dissonance of the people who carried them. The United States stars and stripes waved from hundreds of hands, and adorned thousands of articles of clothing. Others carried flags with Trump's name, flown as fervently as if it were a symbol of the same patriotism. Still others carried a version of a US flag in black and white, with a single blue line bisecting its center, the design intended to show support for the law enforcement rank-and-file with whom the mob's members now engaged in hand-to-hand combat, often using as weapons the flag poles from which those flags were draped.

Others carried Confederate or Don't Tread on Me flags, but those seemed less alternate reality when wielded by insurrectionists intent on overturning an American presidential election.

Perpetrators all, yes, but unwittingly treasonous, these men and women who came from across the US at their president's call. They were also victims. In their minds, they were there to do good. How could they not know that they were doing profound harm to the country they professed to love, a harm that might never be repaired?

How could they not know? How could hundreds of thousands, perhaps many millions who didn't make it to DC to join the insurrection but were there in spirit, be so thoroughly duped?

The man they supported had a longstanding reputation as a swindler. Countless workers and small business-people claimed he'd stiffed them out of the money he owed them for services rendered. He'd fleeced millions more from thousands of students at his so-called Trump University, a "massive scam," according to the conservative publication, *National Review*. Falsehoods slipped from his lips as easily as breath—the *Washington Post* counted more than thirty thousand lies during his four years in office. Trump had been accused of rape twice—once by Ivana Trump, first of his ex-wives—and of other, less serious sexual misconduct multiple times.

Then, there was his blatant bigotry. He'd come to political prominence by suggesting that Barack Obama wasn't really American and had concocted an elaborate scheme to hide his supposed African birthplace. Trump smeared immigrants from Mexico as rapists and drug dealers, winked and nodded at white supremacists, and labeled neo-Nazis "very fine people" after they chanted "Jews will not replace us" at a racist rally.

Those supporting Trump had to know at least some of this history, and some must have known all of it. At minimum, they were not bothered enough to question whether such a character could be trusted.

Perhaps, in a way, as Trump supporters willfully blocked their synapses from connecting to the obvious meaning of such a biography, they were doing the same for their own. Maybe having a crook who could make Archie Bunker blush as their president made everyday prejudices and transgressions seem, not just palatable, but reasonable.

But, at least for some of those gathered, Trump's well-documented distasteful history didn't need to be accepted because they were convinced it was all a lie, part of the plot to bring down the one man fighting to save America from Deep State operatives—including celebrities, evil Democrats, major media elites, and billionaire George Soros—who, they believed, trafficked children in Satanic pedophile rings, and drank their blood in a quest for eternal youth.

This was QAnon, a cult without a religion, whose prophet was Q, a person or persons who claimed to be a high level US intelligence officer. Q's first post, in 2017, promised that Hillary Clinton was imminently due to be arrested. That never happened, but it didn't faze those who became riveted by "Q drops," cryptic messages from Q that invited readers on conspiracy websites to do the research for themselves, and discover that Q's clues were true.

The supposed intel never added up to anything real. Anyone who actually researched beyond conspiracy websites would discover that Q's clues were nonsense. It didn't seem to matter. Members of the Q movement believed they had discovered the truth. They simply knew. Any attempt to dissuade them proved the attempted dissuader was part of the Deep State plot.

Whenever Trump called some piece of information that was un-favorable to him "fake news"—for instance, Biden's winning the presidency—it looked to those immersed in the Q movement like further evidence of the wide-ranging power of the cabal, not evidence that Trump was simply lying. Those who attached themselves to QAnon accepted that the Deep State would do anything to stop Trump from taking down their cabal, and would tell the most outrageous falsehoods about him to try to turn patriots against him. But "the Storm" was coming. Trump had a plan to arrest all the Deep State actors; some would be executed on the spot. The date of the storm, to many QAnon adherents, was January 6th.

For whatever reason—whether the mass delusion of QAnon, or garden variety bigotry and misogyny, or identification with Trump's complaints of persecution and grievance, or worry that the country was changing too rapidly—millions believed in Trump. And thousands were pumped up enough by this man to travel to Washington, DC,from all across the United States, to commit crimes on his behalf. They were down the rabbit hole, through the looking glass, use any Lewis Carroll analogy. It would fit.

Because of the rally and multiple adjunct demonstrations around the city, Capitol staff had advised members of Congress to arrive at the complex by tunnel, passing under the streets immediately surrounding the buildings. That route, which had brought Congresswoman Susan Wild to an underground parking garage earlier in the day, meant she didn't see the hordes of Trump supporters amassing around the Capitol campus during her five-minute drive from her apartment to her office in the Longworth House Office Building. Along the way, she saw street hawkers selling Trump-themed souvenirs, but little hint of the enraged masses gathering elsewhere.

Once parked in the garage, she used pedestrian tunnels to get to her office. With no visual alerts to signal the danger boiling just across the street, Wild's focus was on the certification. Her Republican colleagues' planned objections seemed more like kabuki than a genuine attempt to overturn the election. She was scheduled to speak in a few hours in reply. In the meantime, after finishing up some work, she headed to the House chamber to observe.

Normally, that would mean taking a seat on the House floor but with the pandemic raging, in Congress, as everywhere else, people had to maintain six feet of distance between them. Those who were due to speak or had other roles that required they be on the floor, were spaced around the cavernous room on the semi-circular padded benches. Those who weren't immediately slated to speak, but wanted to watch the proceedings, had to sit in the gallery. Pre-pandemic, this upper section, with its bird's-eye view of the floor, hosted only members of the visiting public and the press. It was laid out like a theater balcony with fold up seating and brass handrails slanting down the steps between the rows every five or six seats.

At 1:00 pm, Vice President Pence, either unaware that the Capitol grounds had been breached, or unaware of how violent the mob was, arrived at the House chamber from the Senate. A contingent of senators followed, to begin the joint session during which the electoral votes from each state would be certified.

Following alphabetical order, first came Alabama, then Alaska. The vice president, officiating over the count in his capacity as the president of the Senate, asked for objections. None were presented. Next came Arizona. Senator Amy Klobuchar, the Democratic teller from the Senate, announced the results in a pro forma declaration.

"Mr. President, the certificate of the electoral vote of the State of Arizona seems to be regular in form and authentic, and it appears therefrom that Joseph R. Biden, Jr, of the State of Delaware, received eleven votes for President and Kamala D. Harris, of the State of California, received eleven votes for Vice President."

Reading from his own set script, Pence replied, "Are there any objections to counting the certificate of vote of the State of Arizona that the teller has verified appears to be regular in form and authentic?"

As expected, Congressman Paul Gosar (R-AZ) stood to object. The slender congressman, whose long red tie looked like a cast-off from Trump's own wardrobe, said that he spoke for himself and sixty other Republican congressional representatives.

In order for the objection to be recognized and debated, it needed the signature of a senator, as well.

Senator Ted Cruz (R-TX), sitting next to Gosar, rose to say he had signed the objection, and that seven other Republican senators would also object. At that point, following the procedure laid out for such a situation, the vice president called for the two Houses to withdraw from the joint session of Congress to separately debate.

Pence and the senators left the House floor; staffers lifted the leather-strapped mahogany cases that contained the certified electoral college ballots, and hauled them back to the Senate. None of this would change the fact that Joe Biden won Arizona. Its eleven electoral votes were certain to be counted for him. The objections simply slowed the process.

Due to pandemic social distancing requirements, the three dozen or so congressional representatives observing from the gallery were sparsely scattered across the area, along with members of the press.

Among the reps sharing the gallery with Susan Wild included her friend and fellow Pennsylvania Democrat, Madeleine Dean; former Army Ranger Jason Crow (D-CO); Pramila Jayapal (D-WA), leader of the Progressive Caucus and on crutches due to a recent knee surgery; former CIA officer Abigail Spanberger (D-VA); former police chief Val Demings (D-FL); Jimmy Gomez (D-CA) and Norma Torres (D-CA).

Earlier, the Capitol Police had texted everyone that there was a large gathering of protesters on the Capitol grounds, but everyone had expected protests, so it wasn't a particularly alarming message.

Although seated too far apart to chat, Susan Wild exchanged surprised glances and hushed titters with colleagues as, below them on the House floor, freshman Congresswoman Lauren Boebert (R-CO) began a decidedly odd objection speech:

> *"Thank you, Madam Speaker. And to ease everyone's nerve I want you to all know that I am not here to challenge anyone to a duel like Alexander Hamilton or Aaron Burr..."*

Boebert, owner of a bar called The Shooters Grill in Rifle, Colorado, where she encouraged her employees to open-carry their weapons while serving the clientele, had been sworn in as a member of Congress just three days before after campaigning, unsurprisingly, on a gun rights platform. She'd spoken favorably of the QAnon conspiracy, and had tweeted that morning that "Today is 1776."

Boebert's speech, riddled with gaffes and malapropisms, caused plenty of eye-rolling during the five minutes she had the floor, serving up the comic relief in an otherwise unsurprising debate.

Meanwhile, another text came through, warning of a breach of the exterior perimeter. Wild wondered, with a touch more concern than she'd felt previously: what was that supposed to mean?

Boebert's speech would provide the last chuckle of the day.

It was still morning in Los Angeles, and screenwriter Patrick Cunnane was watching Senate Majority Leader Mitch McConnell (R-KY) on TV, giving an impassioned speech on the Senate floor. McConnell was saying all the right things, and although Pat never once doubted that Biden would be inaugurated, after the craziness of Trump's attempts to overthrow the election for the last couple of months, it was a relief to hear the majority leader inject some sanity into the process:

"My colleagues, nothing before us proves illegality anywhere near the massive scale—the massive scale—that would have tipped the entire election. Nor can public doubt alone justify a radical break, when the doubt itself was incited without any evidence. The constitution gives us here in Congress a limited role. We cannot simply declare ourselves the national board of elections on steroids. The voters, the courts, and the states have all spoken. They've all spoken. If we overrule them, it would damage our republic forever."

It was probably the only time in memory when Pat found himself agreeing wholeheartedly with McConnell.

Tall, lean, and boyishly handsome, Pat Cunnane, 33, came from a politically active family in Pennsylvania. He'd arrived in Hollywood by way of Pennsylvania Avenue, working his way up, over six and a half years, from intern to senior writer in the Obama White House. His proud parents, Patrick and Madeleine Cunnane, were so excited for him, they'd accompanied him to Washington, DC, on his first day.

Penning op-eds, talking points, and even a comedy sketch for President Obama with comedian Jerry Seinfeld, gave Pat the perfect background, when the Obama years were done, to join the screenwriting team for the TV show *Designated Survivor*.

But if he had left DC behind, his politically active family hadn't. His mom, Madeleine, was now doing her own star turn in Washington, DC, having won election in 2018 as congresswoman for Pennsylvania's fourth district. She served under her maiden name, Madeleine Dean.

Pat, three thousand miles away, still spoke to his mom almost daily.

Although he had yet to see any violence as he watched the news reports, he became concerned about her being recognized by the crowds of Trump supporters outside the Capitol and called one of her staffers.

"'Hey, what's the plan for her leaving the Capitol. I don't want her to walk through alone." The staffer told him that there was indeed a plan in place, and she would be safe.

A moment later, one of his old college roommates texted Pat that news stations were reporting a bomb threat near the Capitol. Quickly, he called his mom, but she assured him that he had nothing to worry about. All was well.

That was about to change.

By 1:30 pm, the building was surrounded on all sides by rioters, but none had yet gotten inside. An older man in a red MAGA hat grabbed one end of the plastic netting that fenced the perimeter, trotting along as he peeled it away as easily as a length of painter's tape.

On the grounds, it was pandemonium. Officers, pushed back by the insurrectionists, could only protect the entrances and egress points to the building itself. All perimeter barricades were down, often re-deployed by the mob as weapons and ladders.

Commander Glover decided to escalate to more powerful munitions, launching large canisters of tear gas into the crowds. It barely slowed them. Dozens at the front of the mob hoisted an enormous Trump 2020 sign encased in a metal frame. Holding it flat, parallel to the ground, they heaved the sign's metal frame against the officers, forcing a break in their line of defense.

Others, having climbed the inaugural scaffolding, pelted the cops from above with sticks, bottles, fire extinguishers, pieces of the scaffold itself—whatever they could find. On the ground, insurrectionists shot thick streams of bear spray and other chemicals at the defenders of the building, many of whom by now, were injured. The same scene replayed, over and over: an officer would be sprayed in the face with mace or another chemical and retreat behind the line to wash the burning substance out of his eyes with bottled water. He'd return to the line just as another, overcome by chemical irritant spray, was forced back.

Glover's men would not be able to hold the line much longer by themselves.

He frantically shouted into his radio to the police joint operations center, for the sixth or seventh time.

"I need those two other hard platoons up here now!"

Officer Daniel Hodges, of the MPD's Civil Disturbance Unit 42, had been stationed at Constitution Avenue since 7:30 am, keeping watch on the crowds that poured toward the Ellipse for Trump's speech, and then out again as it ended. Many were decked out in wild and silly costumes. But Hodges also noted an unusual number in battle gear: ballistic vests, helmets, military face masks, tactical boots, and radios equipped with earpieces. These weren't what people wore just to listen to politicians speak in a park. Moments after word came over his radio of an undetonated bomb being handled by the explosive ordinance disposal team, his orders changed: don "hard gear" and head to the Capitol's west terrace.

He suited up in the police van along with others in his unit. Demonstrators were sparse at the northwest edge of the Capitol grounds, but got denser the closer they came to the building. The crowd booed and heckled the cops, yelling "Traitor," as they passed, single file, with hands on the shoulders of the officer in front.

And then, at about 2:00 pm, as Hodges' unit reached the edge of the inauguration scaffolding, the mob turned violent.

They surged at the cops, surrounding them, pummeling them with fists, flagpoles, and makeshift weapons. Hodges noted with a mix of irony and horror that among the flags attached to the poles with which they beat his brothers in blue was the one with a thin blue line, the symbol of support for law enforcement. One guy wrestled Hodges for his baton. He managed to hang onto it, but during the attack, members of his unit were forced apart.

In his mind, he'd been viewing these people as protesters. But protesters didn't attack cops, and they didn't try to overrun their seat of government. Nor did patriots, the name they gave themselves. He had a more accurate label for them: terrorists. He'd been in the military and he knew the difference.

He also recognized that some would likely do anything to stop him and his fellow officers from advancing, even kill them.

A heavy metallic object, thrown down from the scaffolding above, clanged off his helmet, nearly knocking him off his feet. For a moment, he swayed, disoriented. Then, he felt a kick to his chest and did fall.

He was on his hands and knees. His surgical face mask, worn as protection against the virus, was over his eyes, blinding him to his attacker. Fellow officers pulled him to his feet, and together, they charged through the crowd as tear gas, mace, and smoke rose all around.

At last, they reached the police line at the bottom of the west terrace, helping to reinforce MPD defenses as they joined their fellow officers behind a row of short bike racks, lined up into an ever-shifting ad hoc fence. But rioters, several hundred deep, and bent on advancing, forced themselves against the line over and over. Police would not be able to hold them back for much longer.

Hodges' radio was gone. Someone must have stolen it during the melee.

The mob chanted:

"Four more years.

"Four more years.

"Four more years."

A rioter yelled in his face, "Do you think your little pea shooter guns are going to stop this crowd? No, we're going in that building."

The mob surged again. The fence buckled and broke apart. And now, it was hand-to-hand combat. An insurrectionist grabbed Hodges, shoved his thumb into his right eye, and attempted to gouge it out, as Hodges screamed in pain. Somehow, he broke free of the man. A dozen more came after him.

He spotted a large hunting knife in the belt of a rioter. He and other officers tackled the man to the ground and disarmed him, as the man shouted at them indignantly.

But the outnumbered officers had been forced back so far they were now cornered at the southern edge of the western terrace. There was no option left but to retreat.

Hodges followed other officers hustling up the stairs, and found a hallway to rest momentarily, sitting for the first time in hours. The cops passed around bottles of water and he washed the chemical residue of mace and tear gas out of his eyes as well as he could before fitting his gas mask to his face for what he anticipated to be a long battle. The worst was yet to come.

Inside the Capitol, a floor below congressional chambers, House Sergeant-at-Arms Irving was in Senate Sergeant-at-Arms Stenger's office, calling in reinforcements from county and state police forces in Virginia and Maryland. Aides to the Senate majority leader and Senate minority leader arrived, looking for answers about what was being done. Irving told them that it would take an hour or two for the police reinforcements to arrive, and it might be time to consider calling in the National Guard.

The Senate aides were stunned that this hadn't already been in the works and, worse, that Irving still appeared to diddling about making the request.

Meanwhile, on the east side of the Capitol, a man in sweat clothes broke through the line, reached the building, kicked in the three lower panes of a window and punched his fist through several panes above it. He was ready to crawl inside the building before two cops tackled him and pulled him away. Several more officers ran to the site of the breach and lined up in front of it, their riot shields up to keep others back.

Cops handcuffed the would-be intruder but unable to connect to anyone in command for instructions about what to do with arrestees, they released him back into the crowd.

The horror of the day etched the officers' expressions: stunned, determined, exhausted, and for some, resigned. The unthinkable had happened, was happening at this very moment, and they had no way to stop it. By one estimate, the ever-swelling horde of insurrectionists now outnumbered cops almost sixty to one.

The metal scaffolding for the inaugural stage and bleachers, installed on the wide stairs of the west side of the Capitol, made much of the staircase on that side of the building unusable. But an entry tunnel was built within the scaffolding itself. It allowed ordinary use of a portion of the stairs, about eight feet across. A mere handful of officers were stationed there.

This relatively undefended entry would give direct access, up past the bleachers, to a terrace section onto which several of the building's windows and doors opened on the Senate side of the building.

Proud Boys and other more aggressive members of the mob attacked, pushing past police, battling them all the way to the next landing where another line of cops attempted to hold them off in a fierce fight.

"He's got a hammer. He's got a hammer!" an officer at the top of the steps called out to his fellow cop, as an insurgent in orange gloves, jeans, and helmet raised the weapon to attack.

In this all-out war, the outnumbered cops were losing. It was a miracle that none yet had been killed.

Though many cops were still fighting off attackers, police command saw the futility and danger of the situation and ordered officers inside the building.

Meanwhile, House Sergeant-at-Arms Irving finally communicated approval to Capitol Police Chief Sund to call in the National Guard.

Up, up through the tunnel opening within the scaffolding the mob stormed, raging, kicking, punching, bludgeoning the last remaining officers along the way. Fellow rioters behind them and to either side cheered them on.

"Take the stairs. Take the stairs."

"Go, go, go, go, go!"

"America! America!"

"We're taking our House back. We're not going to take your fucking vaccine. We're not going to take your bullshit. The people are rising up!"

Hundreds moved up behind the first group. Those inside the scaffolding stepped over or crawled under the structure that blocked most of the staircase. A few hardier individuals climbed the scaffolding itself, using its frame like monkey bars to speed their way to the top. Members at the rear of the group moved more slowly. Most passed unimpeded by the last few officers who had not yet been pulled back inside. Some rioters at the back of the surge might have been unaware of how savage a battle had raged within that passage moments before.

Right-leaning pundits and politicians would later try to paint the entire mob as peaceful. The viciousness of the assaults on police made that claim ludicrous. But it's true not all those in the mob engaged in violence nor were all members of militias, Proud Boys, Three Percenters, or other coordinated groups.

What might be said of those following behind the violent vanguard is that they were sheep led by wolves. When agitators stoked these masses, however, either by intimidating the cops as they stormed past them, or by leading a threatening chant, even the sheep displayed fangs.

A few insurrectionists taunted the straggler cops still on the terrace.

"You know we're right."

"Back off!"

"Fuck the blue."

"Let's go!"

Those in the front line pounded on windows with fists and weapons. A window cracked in a sunburst pattern, but still wouldn't break. Proud Boy Dominic Pezzola, who had earlier stolen a cop's riot shield, heaved it against the glass with all his might. Next to him, another man thrusted a two-by-four at an adjacent pane. Pezzola continued smashing the shield against the glass until the battering forced the compromised pane out of its frame and onto the floor inside.

The building was breached. It was 2:13 pm.

Among the first dozen rioters who climbed in, one carried a Confederate flag—a jaw-dropping image.

Two men kicked at a locked door a few feet from away until it gave. Dozens more poured in. Others shattered a window on the opposite side of the door. More clambered through.

Proud Boy Joe Biggs exclaimed as he entered, "This is awesome." Then, perhaps noticing the multitude of cameras filming the scene, pulled his gaiter up over his face.

The horde followed, swarming to the left and right. A massive group streamed into the Crypt, a large columned room beneath the Rotunda with arched ceilings.

"We are in the Capitol, baby."

"USA. USA. USA. USA."

"Whose House?"

"Our House."

"Whose House?"

"Our House."

"Trump, Trump, Trump, Trump, Trump, Trump, Trump, Trump."

4

Trapped

"Break it down. Break it down. Break it down. Break it down."

— Insurrectionists battering the doors to the House chamber

S ecret Service agents, learning that the building had been penetrated, hustled Vice President Pence off the Senate dais at about 2:13 pm, just two minutes after rioters first broke the window on the upper west terrace and one minute after rioters began climbing through to the inside. Pence, his family, and the rest of his entourage were temporarily secreted in an office just off the legislative body's floor. The Senate abruptly gaveled into recess, cutting off Senator James Lankford (R-OK) mid-objection speech. An exasperated Senator Mitt Romney (R-UT) yelled at his fellow Republicans who had supported Trump's Big Lie. "This is what you've gotten, guys."

Senators began evacuating their chamber.

Not so, at the House.

The roar of the crowd surrounding the Capitol had reverberated through the halls for most of the day. But the first breach occurred on the Senate side of the massive building, the equivalent of a good city block away from the House chamber. Most House lawmakers apparently assumed that whatever was going on was still limited to outside the building.

Congresswoman Norma Torres (D-CA), who had been in the House gallery to watch the counting of the electoral ballots, stepped out to use the restroom, one flight down. When she returned, she saw plain clothes security team members trotting back and forth in the hallway. She'd been a 911 dispatcher for many years, and listened to the chatter coming from their radios for keywords that would tell her what was going on, but couldn't make out what was said.

The shouting and screaming outside now seemed to be getting louder. It didn't occur to her that the shouting might be coming from inside.

A plain clothes officer hustled her back into the gallery, and she took her seat.

A text from the Capitol Police came through on Congresswoman Susan Wild's phone: the inner perimeter had been breached.

She had always felt that the Capitol was the safest place on earth. This was where the Congress of the United States met. Everything in the government's power would be done to protect them; she wouldn't allow herself to panic. But if the situation escalated, would help arrive in time?

Below the gallery, floor staff reassured the lawmakers: Everything was all right. Under control.

The debate continued.

Congresswoman Wild barely heard Paul Gosar (R-AZ) giving his objection speech on the House floor, claiming once again, despite the conspiracy theory having been widely debunked, that rigged Dominion voting machines had stolen the election from Trump. She was busy looking for a place to hide, should one be needed. She decided to make her way over to the press box, where she could duck under one of the press tables if rioters broke in.

Down on the House floor, protective detail officers told Speaker Pelosi's floor director Keith Stern that they had to get the speaker off the floor.

"Let's make it look normal," Stern said. He had already alerted Congressman Jim McGovern (D-MA) that the speaker might need a break and asked him to take the gavel. Within seconds, officers had Speaker Nancy Pelosi (D-CA), Majority Leader Steny Hoyer (D-MD), and other members of the House leadership out of the chamber and off to a secure location.

McGovern hadn't been paying attention to the news. He'd gotten the text that there were rioters in the building, but assumed it was at most, a handful of people, who had somehow gotten past security and were hollering up a storm. In the immense building, sounds echoed. Pelosi thanked him as she left and he thought she said she'd be right back. She'd left her phone, so McGovern had no reason to believe she wouldn't be.

Suddenly, everything got noisier—voices rising, doors slamming or banging—McGovern wasn't quite sure what he was hearing, but he still wasn't particularly worried.

Gosar, still speaking and looking annoyed at the cacophony that was filtering onto the floor demanded: "Mr. Speaker, can I have order in the chamber?"

Security told McGovern to adjourn the proceedings. Not understanding the situation, instead, McGovern declared the House in a short recess at 2:18 pm, just as a text alert from the Capitol Police went out to staff: "Due to security threat inside: immediately, move inside your office, take emergency equipment, lock the doors, take shelter."

Voices rose in concern around the House floor.

A text came in to McGovern from his daughter: "Where are you now?"

He texted back: "I'm in the speaker's chair."

She replied: "I know you are, but why are you there?"

The daughter, watching events unfold on TV, assumed he understood the danger he was in. The father had no clue.

The Crypt was, by 2:21 pm, flooded with rioters. A sparse row of Capitol Police officers formed a line in front of the much larger mob in an attempt to keep them contained. The stand-off seemed almost friendly, at first, with members of the force, and of those carrying flags and wearing Trump paraphernalia of every description, speaking to one another without apparent rancor or aggression. A moment later, someone in the back began a one-word chant:

"Trump, Trump, Trump, Trump, Trump, Trump, Trump, Trump."

The chant grew in intensity, volume and hostility. And then, a shout: "Let's go!" and a solid wall of insurrectionists rushed the cops, surrounding them, assaulting them, and overpowering them.

"Trump, Trump, Trump, Trump, Trump. USA! USA! USA!"

Anyone who hesitated in the surge forward would have been trampled. Some found themselves carried forward in the mad frenzy, their feet no longer contacting the floor.

Officer James Blassingame, one of the eight or nine cops forced backward by the rioters' surge, got slammed against one of the Crypt's stone columns. Unable to move as rioters battered the cop over almost every part of his body with fists, bottles, flagpoles, and other bludgeons, Blassingame was almost as stunned by the countless times they hurled the N-word at him. "We'll fuck you up if you don't get out of our way."

He couldn't if he wanted to. He was pinned.

The assault seemed endless; the threats grew in hostility. "Get down or I'll put you down," one rioter screamed. Blassingame assumed he wasn't getting out of there alive.

But, at last, the injured officer was able to pull himself free, as the throng spread out, pouring into hallways, staircases, expanding to fill the space.

"USA! USA! USA! USA! USA! USA!"

MPD Police Chief Contee had just returned from assessing the scene at the Capitol when a conference call was convened at 2:22 pm with officials at the Pentagon, DC officials, General Walker, Chief Sund, and himself.

Walker had tried to get Secretary of the Army Ryan McCarthy on the call, but was told he was with acting Secretary of Defense Christopher Miller and was unavailable.

His voice cracking with emotion, Chief Sund pleaded with the generals. "I am making an urgent, urgent immediate request for National Guard assistance. I have got to get boots on the ground."

Contee expected the Pentagon response to be, '*Yes, the National Guard is responding. Yes, the National Guard is on the way. Yes, the National Guard are being restaged from traffic posts to respond.*' But that wasn't close to what happened.

Instead, while police were being overwhelmed by thousands of insurrectionists at the seat of government, the Pentagon officials dithered. They hemmed and hawed.

Well, what was the plan for the National Guard? they wanted to know. *What about the optics? How would it look to have boots on the ground in the Capitol?*

One of the generals on the call said he would run the request up the chain of command at the Pentagon. But he was inclined to advise against it.

Chief Contee was stunned. He had officers who were literally fighting for their lives, and the military brass weren't sure they wanted to get involved?

Contee interjected, so there would be no doubt: "Chief Sund, are you requesting the National Guard?"

"Yes," replied Sund. Yes, of course, he was.

"And is that request being denied?" he asked the generals.

"No, we're not denying the request," one of them replied. But neither were they in any rush to help.

Still assuming that the sounds he was hearing were the shouts of a few errant protesters who'd soon be rounded up, McGovern called the chamber back to order at 2:21 pm, three minutes after the recess, and allowed Gosar to resume his speech.

Gosar moved down his list of wild conspiracy theories, claiming that thirty-thousand undocumented immigrants had voted in Arizona. A security official with the sergeant-at-arms staff approached to tell McGovern it was no longer safe; they were going to have to evacuate the chamber. Then the official took the mic at the rostrum and announced to all at 2:29 pm that the House was in lockdown.

As floor staff gestured to all those in the chamber to stay seated, the official at the mic told those inside: The building had been breached. But everything was fine.

Clearly, only one of those two statements could be true.

Up in the gallery, where Susan Wild and other Democratic representatives were seated, the doors to the hallway had been left open to allow for ventilation. Security personnel began running down the halls, slamming the doors.

From somewhere on the House floor, they heard a boom, and what looked like smoke seeped under one of the doors. Tear gas.

A stocky plain clothes officer appeared on the dais: "Please grab a mask," he said, referring to the gas masks under their seats. "Place it on your lap. And be prepared to don your mask."

Wild hadn't even known there were gas masks under there, and had no idea how to put hers on. From another part of the gallery, a distraught and angry Dean Phillips (D-MN) bellowed down to Gosar and the other Republicans on the floor: "This is because of *you!*"

Though some in the gallery tried to hush Phillips, his friend and colleague, Congressman Tom Malinowski (D-NJ), was with him one hundred percent. If not for all the Republican lawmakers voicing specious objections to certification, thus giving heft to Trump's Big Lie, would a mob be trying to force its way in at this moment, convinced that there was, indeed, a "steal" to stop? Phillips was right, but it surprised his friend that he, of all people, would shout it out; Phillips had strong friendships with members in both parties.

Earlier, Malinowski and Phillips had left the chamber for a while so they could look out the windows at the thousands converging on the building. A Capitol officer rushed over and said, please step away from the windows. Phillips, alarmed by what he was seeing asked her, "Are we safe here?"

The officer reassured them, "Look guys, you're in the United States Capitol, probably the safest building in America, if not the world."

That satisfied Malinowski.

Like so many others, he assumed that the security they could see wasn't close to everything they had, probably just a small part of an overwhelming protective force guarding the nation's Capitol. Those forces, both visible and hidden, would be able to tackle whatever got thrown at them—or so Malinowski believed.

He was just now learning how wrong he'd been.

Capitol Police and sergeant-at-arms' staff had slammed the doors to the hall, but couldn't immediately lock them because no one could find the keys.

Nobody seemed to know what they were doing.

Congressman Jason Crow (D-CO) had, minutes before, come to the
same conclusion: no one knew what they were doing.

He'd initially had confidence that the Capitol Police would be up to
the task of handling any Trump supporters who tried to force their
way past the perimeter fences or even beyond. And Capitol Police civil
disturbance units were indeed trained in handling unauthorized people
or groups who attempted to enter the building. But they had never
been trained to deal with a storming of the building by insurrectionists,
some not only armed but communicating with each other via hand
signals and radio.

Though Crow hadn't been concerned about security at the Capitol,
itself, he and his wife had decided it would be better if she took the
kids back home to Colorado a couple of days early, just in case things
got ugly in the surrounding city.

Unlike some of his colleagues, while seated in the gallery, Crow had
been following news reports closely on his phone and saw things get
ugly right outside. Swarms of protesters easily knocked down the
barricades and violently confronted what looked like, at best, a few
hundred police. The cops couldn't defend their positions. They kept
getting pushed back. Could they defend Congress?

Those in the gallery were only supposed to observe for an hour each
and then head out, to give the next group a turn. He knew from what
he was viewing online that it wouldn't be safe to go back to their offices,
but still didn't appreciate the extent of the danger until the order came
up from the floor to get their gas masks.

Now, he had to reassess. The situation was descending into chaos.

It had been about fifteen years since Crow had served as an Army
Ranger. He'd seen battle as a platoon leader in Iraq. He'd also worn gas
masks countless times in the military, both in training and in battle,

but some of his colleagues had never seen the apparatus before. He set his mind on showing them how to prepare the masks and how to put them on, but told those near him to hold off on putting the masks on until they smelled gas. Wearing the masks too long could make someone hyperventilate and even pass out.

Police began evacuating lawmakers who were on the floor, but it seemed to Crow that they were unaware of the two dozen or so representatives and the dozen members of the press in the gallery. Crow's friend and colleague, Congresswoman Diana DeGette (D-CO) apparently had the same thought and yelled down to the police on the floor: "What about us?'

If there was a response, Crow didn't hear it. He was looking at news and social media reports on his phone again at one of the most shocking scenes he could remember seeing: the mob had fanned out around the building. Insurrectionists were encircling the House chamber.

But a moment later, he wouldn't need his phone to appreciate the grim situation. A booming sound rose up from one of the doors on the House floor below, a sound so loud, it could have been made by a battering ram. They were trying to break down a door in the back of the chamber, one that opened to the House floor from near the Statuary Hall. He got up and checked that the gallery doors were now, indeed, locked.

Markwayne Mullin (R-OK) could tell almost immediately that the security personnel in the chamber were not trained for the situation they were in. A moment before, one had told lawmakers to lie down on the floor.

"Do not lay down on the floor," he stood up and shouted to his colleagues. "If they hit that door, we need to go out those doors and down those steps."

Lying down during a riot would get people killed, he explained to the plain clothes officer. They'd get stomped.

Rioters had begun pounding on the first of two sets of doors that led into the back of the chamber. And Mullin, a former mixed martial arts fighter, realizing that security forces were shorthanded, jumped in to help. He and a guard grabbed a desk and shoved it against the door. Someone else hefted a padded bench on top of it. All around him, lawmakers were fumbling with gas masks they had no idea how to wear. And the rioters kept pounding.

Seconds later, from the sound of it, the mob had forced their way through the first set of doors and were attacking the second set, the ones that would give them direct entry into the chamber.

As colleagues hurried to follow evacuation instructions through the door at the front of the House, several lawmakers joined Mullin and the plain clothes cops to defend the door at the back. Troy Nehls was a former sheriff. Tony Gonzales and Ronny Jackson were US Navy veterans. Pat Fallon had served in the Air Force. All were from Texas. All were freshmen who had been sworn in for the first time just days before. And all were Republicans. Andrew Clyde (R-GA), also stayed behind to offer his assistance to police as others evacuated.

Because the white glass of the doors that opened into the chamber was opaque, the Capitol security forces and their lawmaker helpers couldn't see how many were on the other side. They didn't know whether there were three or three hundred; the latter was closer to the truth. However many there were, Mullin didn't believe they could keep them out indefinitely. But they could buy time, and time would let others in the chamber escape.

"Are we doing this, brother?" said Troy Nehls.

"I'm with you brother," Mullin replied.

Up in the gallery, an officer was preparing to evacuate the lawmakers and media people trapped there. They opened a door by the clock tower and an officer shouted "Get up. Go, go, *go!*"

Several of those closest to the door got out, including Malinowski and Phillips, and guided by Capitol police officers, made their way to an elevator.

Moments later, at approximately 2:37 pm, from the House chamber floor came a bang and a voice yelling, "Shots fired. Shots fired. Everyone down!"

The escape door from the gallery slammed shut again with most of the representatives and media still trapped inside.

Madeleine Dean called her husband, PJ Cunnane, then her son, Pat.

Over the phone, Pat could hear yelling and banging in the background. His mom was clearly upset but kept trying to reassure him. He could hear someone tell her to put on her gas mask.

He put the call on speaker and his wife joined the conversation, sounding just as upset as his mom. But all he could feel at the moment, besides fear for her safety, was anger. It was what he imagined a call from a loved one during a school shooting would be like.

He wouldn't allow himself to consider that it might be the last time he would ever speak to her.

Within moments, she had to go, but promised she would call back when she was safe.

They said their I love yous, but stopped short of saying those dreaded words: *'If anything should happen...'*

She would be all right, she said.

Madeleine Dean didn't share the image that had been burning itself into her psyche of the doors being thrown open by the terrorists on the other side, or of the AR-type guns she imagined spraying across the gallery and the floor.

No. She couldn't do that to them. She told them that she loved them. And she would be all right. Then, over her head, she pulled on the plastic bag apparatus of the gas mask.

When rioters broke through the opaque white glass of the back door into the chamber that Markwayne Mullin and the Texas freshmen were helping to guard, it sounded like a gunshot.

Capitol Police drew their guns, yelling at once, "Shots fired, shots fired."

Mullin thought so, too, until he realized the sound was of the glass being punched. He hollered back, "No shots. Don't fire. Don't shoot!"

Through the broken window, they could see a man with a flag on a pole. The pole had been sharpened to a point, most likely what had punched through the glass.

As the cops lowered their weapons, Mullin yelled at the insurgents, "Is it worth it? You almost got killed. Is it worth it?"

For a moment, there was silence. Then a voice from the other side shouted, "This is our House," as he pushed his face closer and began shaking the door again. "This is our fucking House and we're taking it back."

"It's our House, too," Mullin shouted back.

And no way was he going to let the rioters take it, not without a fight.

Although it wasn't a shot that punched through the glass, the compromised door window in the back of the House chamber meant it was no longer safe to evacuate the gallery. The opening in the broken window gave rioters on the other side of the glass a direct sightline to the entire back of the gallery. Capitol officers told everyone to take cover.

Jason Crow's first thought was to try to secure the perimeter. His second was to get the members together in a small group. If they had to fight for their lives—and it seemed increasingly likely that that would be so— they needed to be together in a tight group that they could defend.

He took out his phone, called his wife, and told her he loved her.

He pulled no punches. They were surrounded, he said. They might have to make a stand in the gallery. They might have to fight their way out.

Whatever happened, he said to tell the kids that he loved them.

It was a call no one should have to make and no wife should have to hear.

She took in what he said and replied: Remember that you're a father. You're a husband and a father. You have obligations to your family. Don't be a hero.

He listened, and reassured her as best he could. Then, he hung up, and got into combat mode. Realizing that lawmakers were "high value" targets, he told his colleagues to take off the pins that identified them as members of Congress. He searched for anything he could use as a weapon. All he had was a pen. Grabbing it from his pocket, he told the other gathered lawmakers to get their pens out, and be prepared to use them as weapons, too.

At about 2:40 pm, a shout went out to the mob jamming close to the door into the back of the chamber from a rioter filming the storming of the Capitol for Infowars.

"There's going to be an emergency evacuation. Right now!"

Forget this door, he told them. House members were escaping through a door on the other side.

"Go, go, go, go!" shouted another one of the insurrectionists, urging the mob to follow. A mass of people began running, turning right, down a narrow hall, then right again. Several insurgents directed the mob into the arched passage that led to the doors of the Speaker's Lobby.

Near the front of this group was a slim, attractive dark-haired woman in her mid-thirties. If you didn't know the context, the way she hopped up and down as she peered through the window, and yelled at the cop in front of her while poking her finger in the air near his face might remind you of an angry coach yelling at the umpire over a bad call. But the "bad call" in this case was that, on the other side of the glass, members of Congress, who she and the rest of the mob hoped to chase down, were getting away.

Just three cops in patrol uniforms stood guard in front of the glass-topped doors that were barricaded on the opposite side by a few chairs and a table.

Several men took turns attacking the glass on either side of the cops' heads. They kicked. They pounded with fists, wood, a helmet. The frame of the doors bent inward as the bulletproof glass cracked, but still did not yield. Neither did the cops, who stood stoically at their posts.

Over her jeans and long-sleeved t-shirt, the petite woman who had been hopping up and down wore a floor-length Trump flag, tied around her neck like a super-hero's cape, with an American flag backpack strapped over it. At first glance, Ashli Babbitt looked to be one of the least threatening people at the Speaker's Lobby doors. But looks, as the cliché goes, can be deceiving. Babbitt, 35, had spent most of her adult life as a soldier. She'd served four years on active duty in the Air Force, two years in the Air Force Reserves, and almost six more in the Air National Guard. Her military duties were, essentially, those of a cop, including riot control; she had been trained to use a club and shield to break up civil disturbances. Another way of looking at it was that most of Ashli Babbitt's adult life involved training and preparation to do violence.

It didn't end with the military. Her first civilian job was in security for a nuclear power plant, where she met Aaron Babbitt, the man who she would later marry. It was during this time that she would repeatedly ram her car into that of her new beau's ex-girlfriend while shouting

TRAPPED

threats. The shaken and fearful ex was granted a restraining order.

So, although this small woman in the silly outfit might, at first, look harmless, she was anything but. Added to all that, she was an avid QAnon follower whose social media accounts made clear she believed all kinds of crazy conspiracy theories about Democrats and others, including that they were getting away with child rape and murder.

What might such a person do if she came face-to-face with those she was determined to catch, the congressional reps who were escaping, just on the other side of the glass doors?

The scene was set for a tragedy. The big question at that point: who would be the victim?

Congressman McGovern hurried out alongside Keith Stern, Pelosi's floor manager, through the doors to the left of the three-tiered dais, toward the Speaker's Lobby, a hallway on the other side of the wall.

It took a while to get through the doorway. Everyone on the floor was trying to exit at once. As he did, he glanced down the hall to the other end of the Speaker's Lobby where he heard loud voices, and was aghast at what he saw through the door glass. The crowd there was enormous. When they saw the congress members, they pounded on the glass above the doors, trying to break through to reach the lawmakers before they could get away. All that stood between the representatives and the rioters, thirty feet away, were three officers on the opposite side of the door, and a pile of chairs on the inside, pushed against the door's bottom.

McGovern was stunned by the rage in their faces. The hate.

Turning to Stern, he said, "These people aren't here to make a political statement. They are here to hurt us." Finally appreciating the peril, he might have been saying it as much to himself as to Stern.

For what seemed like an eternity, but was probably only seconds, he gazed at those angry faces. Then he joined the others as police rushed them through another doorway and down the stairs.

A man in the crowd at the Speaker's Lobby doors shouted at the cops: "Go home. We don't want to hurt you."

It was clear from the bloody path the insurrectionists had left along the way that these three could quickly join the list of casualties.

A chant roared up from others crammed into the hallway.

"Break it down."

"Break it down."

"Break it down."

"Break it down."

They wanted their prey. And their prey were getting away.

Amid the sea of red MAGA hats in the hallway behind Ashli Babbitt was a man with long hair, a long grey beard, and a hooded sweatshirt decorated with a skull and text that read "Camp Auschwitz." In block letters on the back of the shirt was one word: "Staff."

From up the stairs at the edge of the hallway, four officers in riot gear, rifles pointed outward, approached. A rioter, seeing the guns, put his hands up, but the officers ignored him and moved forward.

One of the cops at the door told the other two, "They're ready to roll," presumably referring to the riot gear squad. Then the three who had been guarding the door moved to the side, eliminating the only barrier between the mob and the doors.

The savagery with which the insurrectionists attacked the glass once the cops moved away seemed a harbinger of what would happen to those fleeing if they caught them. One man, wearing a fur hat with flaps, and dressed in a black shirt with yellow accents—a type shirt often worn by Proud Boys—kicked so hard, the whole door shook. Others joined in, pounding with fists, and a helmet. The fur-hatted guy grabbed the helmet away from the man using it and continued to batter the glass in the doors and the narrow windows on either side of them.

An officer standing guard outside the House chamber on the opposite side of the doors moved further out toward the center of the Speaker's Lobby, his gun out and clearly visible. He shouted a warning to stop or he'd shoot.

One of the mob yelled, "Yo, there's a gun."

Several others near the doors saw it too.

"Gun, *gun!*"

"He's got a gun!"

But it didn't stop or even slow the frenzied pummeling.

From the back of the crowd, the chant rose again.

"Break it down."

"Break it down."

"Break it down."

It was as if members of this mob thought, having forced their way through multiple layers of law enforcement, they were now invincible.

The glass in narrow pane to the right of the doors gave first, then the pane in the left door. Two insurrectionists hoisted Babbitt up. She climbed through the right window frame ready to chase down the escaping lawmakers.

"Break it down."

"Break it down."

"Break it down."

At 2:44 pm, a shot reverberated in the narrow hall, sounding a single *Pow!* that was almost muted by the cacophony of voices.

Babbitt fell backward from the window to the floor with such force, it appeared she'd been shoved. The bullet pierced her throat. The life drained out of her. For a second, a lone voice from the back could still be heard, chanting, *"Break it down, break it…"* trailing off to silence, as the realization struck.

Adrienne Wild hadn't been paying much attention to the news. As a nanny for two little boys in her hometown of Allentown, Pennsylvania, the 24-year-old kept plenty busy. She didn't feel right about checking her phone very often while at work.

She knew there were protesters outside the Capitol. She'd been to the Capitol a few times herself, to visit her mother, Congresswoman Susan Wild. Protests were the norm in the city.

But articles about this particular protest kept pinging her phone. She'd even seen something about someone getting inside the Capitol, but assumed it was one person.

So when texts from people she knew popped up asking, "Are you okay?" "Is your mom okay?" she answered yes, but didn't think much about it.

A notification came through on her phone that her mom, Susan Wild, was starting a Facetime session for the family. Joining the call with her brother Clay, she got her first inkling that something was very wrong. Adrienne could tell that her mom was somewhere in the Capitol building, but didn't understand why she was in such an unnatural position, her hair swinging down to the sides. She seemed to be hunched over her phone. And she looked scared—more than scared. She looked frantic. In the background, Adrienne could hear a commotion: shouting, glass breaking, and a blur of loud, unidentifiable noise.

Rushing to the garage so that the two children she cared for wouldn't hear any of their conversation, she expected to learn what was happening, but almost all that her mom said was, "I just wanted to call to tell you I love you. And everything is going to be fine."

"How can you be fine?" her brother Clay almost shouted into the phone. "We heard gunshots."

Susan had always been a rock, just unbelievably strong. That might have been what scared Adrienne most. Her mom unfailingly held it together. Yet, here she was, clearly falling apart. And the whole country might be falling apart with her.

Before her mother could end the call, Adrienne quickly took a screenshot of her face. She sensed it might be the last time she saw her alive.

The call from his mom lasted less than a minute but was devastating. Clay Wild felt shell-shocked. Earlier in the day, he'd gotten texts from her saying that alerts had come over her phone about sheltering in place. Clay, having worked for Obama all those years was used to such alerts. They never amounted to much.

Seeing her in that Facetime call in such a terrifying position and worse, hearing the banging and screaming and then, the gunshot, he recognized for the first time how perilous her situation was. He cycled through every awful emotion it seemed possible to feel—anxiety, horror, rage, sadness, worry, helplessness—until, much like his former Obama White House colleague, Pat Cunnane, he settled on anger. All of this was happening because one man, Donald Trump, could not wrap his head around losing, and to appease him, his enablers in Congress essentially invited an insurrection on their own House.

Later, Clay would feel grave concern about what this meant for his country. But at that moment, all he could think of was what it meant for his mom.

The news didn't seem to have caught on yet to the extent of the mayhem. He messaged Pat to ask if he knew anything more.

Susan Wild had lost her left shoe while climbing under the brass railings between the rows of seats that turned the seating area into an obstacle course. She'd worried that that would hobble her as they made their escape but she wasn't thinking of escape now. She lay prone on the floor, hand to her chest, finding it difficult to think, to breathe, to function at all. Just the act of calling had completely unnerved her.

Jason Crow rushed to her side. He held her hand, told her he was there for her and wouldn't let any harm come to her.

"We will get through this," he said.

Was that the truth? Crow didn't know.

The House floor was now completely evacuated, except for Mullin and a few officers. Mullin didn't want to leave until the gallery was cleared but Crow persuaded him that staying put the officers in jeopardy, as they would be forced to remain with him. After getting Crow's assurance that he would get everyone out of the gallery safely, Mullin evacuated, too.

A team of police pushed their way through the mob and cleared a path, forcing the rioters who had penetrated the hallway outside the House gallery to lie face-down on the mosaic tile floor. Communicating via radio with the team on the other side of the gallery doors, they directed them to open a door near a staircase flanked by marble pillars. It was time to get the last of those still trapped in the gallery to safety.

Congresswoman Norma Torres removed her gas mask. In truth, it was more like a plastic bag than a mask. It covered her whole head. She could barely breathe with it on. She also couldn't hear the officers' directions because the "mask" made a whirring mechanical noise.

A female officer pointed the way to the door they would be using to evacuate. She asked Torres and the others in her group if they understood. Then she opened the door and told them to run. They hurried out of the gallery and right into a group of men in street clothes rushing toward them. Some in the group screamed; some started praying, thinking these were rioters. But one of the men yelled, "We are your security. We're here to protect you."

Surrounding the group of lawmakers, they led them down the

stairwell.

Just then, Torres's phone rang. It was her son, Chris, a police officer, worried for her safety.

"Sweetheart, I'm fine," she answered. "But I'm running for my life. I cannot talk to you right now."

Susan Wild hadn't realized how much her distress had shown after she Facetimed with her kids. She had never before had a panic attack but realized that that must have been what it was.

Composed now, she got ready for the officer's cue to leave their hiding place. She would have been the last person in the last group exiting the gallery but Jason Crow circled around behind her. Crow had also found and retrieved her shoe; he handed it to her.

Officers gave the go-ahead and they hustled into the hall. Spread-eagled on the floor, about ten feet from them, were several insurrectionists. Cops with their guns drawn kept the rioters still while Wild, Crow and others hurried down the stairwell. Minutes later, they were led into the first of what were deemed secure locations. It was now 2:53 pm.

Soon after the last members were evacuated from the gallery, the first reinforcements began rolling in from neighboring law enforcement agencies. They helped push rioters out of some of the Capitol spaces. But, by this time, perhaps two thousand insurrectionists had breached the building in numerous locations. It was impossible to force them all out until more help arrived.

The National Guard, as yet, was nowhere to be seen.

Astonishingly, acting Secretary of Defense Christopher Miller hadn't even authorized their deployment.

5

Meanwhile, In The Senate

"This will be a stain on our country not so easily washed away—the final, terrible, indelible legacy of the 45th President of the United States and undoubtedly our worst."

— Then-Senate Minority Leader Chuck Schumer

The Senate was sealed at 2:15 pm, at almost the same moment that chaos broke out one floor below. About twenty rioters scurried across the elaborately patterned mosaic floors, chasing a lone Capitol Police officer, Eugene Goodman.

Goodman backed away from the mob, retrieving the collapsible baton he had dropped moments before, and ascended a marble staircase, while a bearded Doug Jensen, 42, led the pursuit. The black t-shirt Jensen wore over his hoodie was adorned with an enormous red, white, and blue letter Q, against a background illustration of an eagle. The shirt identified him as a follower of QAnon, the cult-like group that believed Trump was fighting a secret cabal of Deep State operatives, celebrities, and elite Democrats who, from behind the scenes, held dominion over everything. This cabal, according to Q, also controlled major media, which is why the media refused to report on its adherents' evil deeds, which included child sex trafficking, Satanic worship, and cannibalism.

To a QAnon believer's mind, January 6th was the beginning of the Storm Q prophesied. The cabal was about to be brought to justice.

First, patriots like him had to stop the counting of the ballots. Then, Trump's enemies would be taken down, and Trump would rise as the rightful president for another four years.

Mass arrests would take place. Even public executions. That was the plan.

Trust the plan, Q had told followers.

Jensen trusted.

Not far behind Jensen were Kevin Seefried, holding a pole from which was draped a large Confederate flag—the first to ever be carried into the US Capitol—and Jacob Chansley, also known as the QAnon Shaman. Probably the most recognizable member of the mob, the heavily tattooed Chansley had marched shirtless to the Capitol in the chill January weather holding a long spear with an American flag tied to it, wearing an animal horn and fur headdress, his face painted red, white, and blue.

While marching, Chansley had wailed about the evils of the imaginary cabal. "Drinking their blood," he'd cried, "Eating our babies." Chansley was now convinced that Pence, too, was part of the cabal, due to Trump's harping on the vice president's refusal to help overturn the election. Behind Jensen, the self-proclaimed QAnon Shaman climbed the steps, the objective, presumably within reach.

As florid as their fantasies were, Chansley, Jensen, and other QAnon followers were probably not as dangerous as others in the mob offshoot that Jensen was leading, such as Robert Gieswein, 24, brandishing a baseball bat, and Proud Boy Dominic Pezzola, still carrying the stolen riot shield he'd used to smash the Capitol window.

A member of the militia group Three Percenters, Gieswein, outfitted for battle in a reinforced military-style vest, and army-style helmet, had marched earlier that morning with the Proud Boys; his helmet bore the orange tape that many Proud Boys sported that day. He had assaulted a number of law enforcement officers on the Capitol grounds before intruding through the window just ahead of Pezzola. Three Percenters, an offshoot of another so-called patriot militia, the Oath Keepers, formed in response to Obama's election in 2008, out of a fear that Obama would come for their guns. It morphed into a paramilitary group that considered county sheriffs to be the "supreme law of the land." The group claimed to be committed to pushing back against what it considered federal overreach and tyranny. Somehow though, Three Percenters were pro-Trump, apparently oblivious to the fact that, as president, Trump was the current head of the supposedly tyrannical federal government.

Meanwhile, according to a witness, Proud Boy Pezzola was aligned with a group whose members said they would kill Pence if given the chance.

"Hey, where they counting?" an eager voice from within Jensen's group shouted at Goodman. "Where they counting the votes?"

Goodman continued walking backwards, demanding the insurgents leave.

"Back up. *Back up!*"

The entrance to the Senate chamber was just a few yards to his right. Pence had been temporarily hidden away in his Senate office, next to the chamber. Senators hadn't yet evacuated.

Jensen glanced toward the chamber door. Goodman lightly poked the Q-obsessed leader's shoulder to distract him, luring him left and upward rather than right, toward the Senate and the vice president. The ploy worked; the mob kept after Goodman as the stocky cop, rushing up the marble staircase, called into his radio, "Second floor."

"We're not here for you," Jensen yelled as they pursued the officer. "We're here for the corrupt government."

Again, Goodman pushed lightly at Jensen to keep the rioter focused on him. Still walking backward, past marble pillars and around a corner, he led the group into a room where about eight more Capitol cops streamed in to confront the insurgents.

Realizing they were trapped, a thin man in glasses and a beard angrily protested, "This is fucking wrong. This is our country."

Jensen, far less confrontational when facing a wall of police, seemed to imagine he could persuade the cop whose gold braided cap identified him as a commanding officer. "What's the point of stopping us at this point?"

"This is as far as it's going to get," the officer replied.

"Then, go arrest the vice president," Jensen insisted, as if that were the most reasonable and obvious response in the world.

Behind Jensen, the QAnon Shaman led a couple of the others in a howl-like chant:

"Wha-*oo*! Wha-*oo*!" It captured the madness of the moment better than words.

At 2:24 pm, while gleefully watching the storming of the Capitol unfold on TV, knowing his vice president was inside the building, his life, quite possibly, in danger, Trump tweeted:

> *"Mike Pence didn't have the courage to do what should have been done to protect our Country and our Constitution."*

Might Trump's tweet have further incited a mob whose members had already injured dozens of police officers and had been chanting "Hang Mike Pence"?

Could that have been the point?

Despite entreaties from the Secret Service, Pence had refused to leave his Senate office. But now, the head of his detail insisted. The office wasn't secure. The windows in the door were glass. Insurrectionists were just outside.

At 2:26 pm, Pence relented. He and his retinue were escorted down the back staircase to the concrete loading dock of a garage in the depths of the Capitol while, elsewhere in the building, rioters, including some who had been calling for his execution, fanned out.

In the chamber, senators who had not yet evacuated began phoning loved ones. A call came in on Utah Republican Senator Mike Lee's phone. The caller ID said simply, the White House, which probably meant one of Trump's advisers, perhaps Mark Meadows.

Lee had been coordinating with Meadows, Trump's chief of staff, since soon after the election, in the frantic—but as Lee had recently realized, futile—attempt to keep Trump in power. Initially, he believed it could be done with a fig leaf of legal justification. But the only hope they had of winning, he'd told Meadows, was if a majority of state legislators in several states Biden had won supported Trump's allegations of massive voter fraud. Then, the legislators would have to signal their willingness to overturn the popular vote, de-certify the Biden electors, and appoint a new slate of Trump electors.

After many attempts to persuade legislators to do just that, Lee had had no success. Days before, he'd told Meadows the plan would likely fail and to push it further risked having it backfire badly.

There didn't seem to be anything further to add, but even in the midst of a siege, he wasn't going to ignore a call from the White House. Answering the phone, he was surprised to hear Trump himself on the line.

Lee assumed that meant Trump wanted to persuade him to stay onboard. He no longer planned to object to the certification—an uncomfortable spot to defend when the president calls, no matter how many rioters were on the other side of the door. The noise level in the Senate chamber made it difficult to hear clearly but he thought Trump said "Tommy," not "Mike." Could he be trying to call someone else?

"Mr. President, this is Mike Lee," said the senator.

"No," insisted Trump. "I dialed Tommy's number."

"Mr. President, are you calling for Tommy Tuberville?"

Trump said yes, and Lee, relieved that he wouldn't be forced into an uncomfortable discussion, agreed to find Tuberville for him.

Senator Tuberville (R-AL), a former Auburn University football coach, had just been elected after first defeating Jeff Sessions, Trump's first attorney general, in the Republican primary. The novice politician had kicked off his primary campaign with a radio ad in which he said, "God sent us Donald Trump because he knew we were in trouble." Needless to say, that message earned Tuberville a warm endorsement from Trump, who had long before soured on Sessions. Tuberville was also the first senator to publicly state that he planned to object to certifying Biden's win. And Tuberville was reportedly in one of the hotel "war rooms" with Trump legal and political advisers over the past day or two, where they had been plotting how to turn Trump's electoral loss into a win.

Tuberville and Trump spoke for several minutes, apparently discussing strategy.Finally, the new senator said, "Mr. President, they've taken the vice president out. They want me to get off the phone, I gotta go."

Tuberville later claimed not to recall much about the conversation he had with Trump during those last few moments or how the then-president had responded to the news that Pence had been evacuated.

Capitol police led the lawmakers through the halls, down the steps, into elevators, and on into the basement to a more secure location. With fewer members in the Senate, evacuation was a much quicker process than would soon occur in the House. By 2:32 pm, every senator was out of the room.

A number of the insurgents led by Jensen were forced out of the Capitol building, through the same window they had used to break in. But with limited police resources, it was a classic case of whack-a-mole. Some almost immediately re-entered through other broken windows and doors.

At 2:25 pm, a door on the east side of the building was breached. Officers closed it down but ten minutes later, rioters stormed through those doors again. Soon, they broke through yet another door on the upper west terrace.

Insurrectionists were everywhere. Up to two-thousand-five hundred would eventually stream inside, wandering through the gracious rooms and elegantly arched corridors of the immense building. Massing in the crypt. Marching through the Rotunda. Rummaging through lawmakers' offices.

And one story down, many thousands more amassed outside the lower west terrace tunnel that led from the Capitol to the inaugural stage. The mob forced the MPD officers who had been holding the line all the way back inside that tunnel. But the couple dozen exhausted MPD officers who they viciously and repeatedly attacked held firm, knowing they were the last defense against the Capitol being completely overwhelmed.

With Pence in the secure area in the lower recesses of the building were his wife, his daughter, and several aides, including his Chief

Counsel Greg Jacob. Jacob had joined Pence's team in March 2020, after having last served in the federal government during the George W. Bush administration.

Earlier in the day, before they all left for the Capitol, Trump had tried, one last time, to persuade Pence to help overturn the election. Trump reportedly told him that he could either go down in history as a "patriot" for asserting the unilateral right to set aside electoral votes, or as a "pussy" if he refused.

But Jacob had advised Pence he had no such right. So had a former Department of Justice official under George W. Bush, John Yoo. Yoo was infamous for declaring that the president had the legal right to torture Iraqi detainees, and to wiretap virtually any communications without first getting a warrant, even to eavesdrop on the phone calls of Americans, as long as one party to the call was outside US borders.

Yoo's broad views of presidential authority made other constitutional experts recoil. But overturning an election on the vice president's say-so was beyond anything even Yoo could endorse. He told Pence no. He could not legally do what Trump wanted.

A former federal appeals court judge, J. Michael Luttig, who had clerked in the past both for Antonin Scalia, and former Supreme Court Chief Justice Warren Burger, also advised Pence that a vice president had no such power.

Now, even as Pence hunkered down, his life under threat, Team Trump continued the pressure.

The Trump lawyer who had come up with the plan for Pence to unilaterally refuse to count certain electoral votes, John Eastman, sent an email to Greg Jacob, Pence's chief counsel, stating that, "The 'siege' is because YOU and your boss did not do what was necessary to allow this to be aired in a public way so that the American people can see for themselves what happened."

Eastman appeared, at best, clueless about, and at worst, indifferent to the hell storm Trump and his enablers had unleashed.

Jacob was stunned.

Capitol Police, still stretched thinly inside the building, were trying to push out rioters who had gotten through, hold back more of the mob from the doors and windows, and react to new breaches as they occurred. Guarding already evacuated spaces was lower priority. Insurgents already in the building had the advantage in spaces without a significant law enforcement presence—including the Senate chamber.

The main foyer on the east side of the Capitol, just inside the arched entry at the top of the Capitol steps, is flanked by the two massive, elaborately decorated bronze doors, known as the Columbus Doors, that depict scenes from the explorer's life. Insurrectionists who had entered through the window broken by Dominic Pezzola and the doors and window near it, flowed through the building to the Crypt, then through the Rotunda, and found themselves at this doorway where they confronted the few cops guarding it. Easily pushing the officers out of the way, they opened the doorway from inside. Hundreds of fellow rioters had been trying unsuccessfully to break in through this entrance for at least twenty minutes. Now, they flooded in.

Among those shoving cops aside on the interior of the doors were Ronald Sandlin, 34, of Tennessee. A plump guy in an orange sweatshirt, baseball cap, black glasses, and backpack, Sandlin hoped to sell video footage of his escapades inside the Capitol and strike it rich. Also tussling with the police was one of his traveling companions, Nathan DeGrave, 31, of Las Vegas, Nevada, wearing black tactical gear and a gas mask that obscured his face. The two had come to the Capitol with a third man they'd met online, Josiah Colt, 34, of Ada County, Idaho. The trio had begun planning about two weeks before when Sandlin asked his Facebook friends to join him to "stop the steal" and "stand behind Trump when he decides to cross the Rubicon." The phrase refers to Julius Caesar, who in 49 BC, led his army across the Rubicon River against the orders of the Roman Senate in an act of insurrection. It could be viewed as apt in more than one way. Caesar, as a result, became Rome's dictator, ending the Roman Republic.

On New Year's Eve, DeGrave, after answering Sandlin's call to action, had posted a request on Facebook, asking if someone with either FBI or special forces training would be willing to teach him how to shoot in the next couple of days. He wrote that his request was for "a very patriotic cause."

After overcoming the police guarding the doorway, an offshoot of the mob, including DeGrave, Sandlin, and Colt, began ascending a staircase with a brass and wrought iron bannister. Their apparent goal: to find and stop the lawmakers who were meeting that day to certify the electoral ballots. The rabble chanted as they climbed:

"Treason, treason, treason, treason, treason, treason, treason, treason."

They made their way up to the third floor on the Senate side of the building, winding through hallways, banging on doors, until they spilled into the corridor outside the Senate gallery.

Just three officers manned this elegant corridor with its spring green walls, intricately patterned tile floor, and decorative arched ceilings. The officers had been locking down the Senate gallery's tall French doors when the mob arrived. DeGrave, Sandlin, and several other insurrectionists moved aggressively, lunging at the cops, grabbing the doors, trying to keep them from closing them.

With at least twenty rioters menacing them, the officers backed off down the hall. At 2:44 pm, the same moment that Ashli Babbitt was shot dead as she climbed through the windowed door to the Speaker's Lobby on the other side of the building, hoping to chase down lawmakers, rioters breached the Senate gallery, expecting to confront the vice president and lawmakers.

But Pence and the senators had long since gone.

Anger and confusion sounded in the voices of the insurgents as they entered an empty Senate through the gallery doors.

"Where are they?"

"Where the fuck are they?"

"Where's fucking Nancy Pelosi?"

"Where the fuck is Nancy?"

Some, after finding the chamber empty, walked in and right out again, disappointment evident in their faces. Others eagerly rushed in, anyway. Some, like the man calling for House Speaker Nancy Pelosi, appeared not to know exactly where they were. And some appeared unsure what they should do now that they'd gotten this far.

Josiah Colt walked down the gallery steps to the railing, climbed over the edge, and dangled by his arm for a long moment above the Senate floor. He dropped down near the dais that Vice President Pence had vacated about half an hour before. Sitting in Pence's chair, mistakenly believing it was House Speaker Pelosi's, he yelled, "Trump won that election."

It's not clear who or how, but someone, perhaps Colt, opened a door into the chamber itself, and a couple dozen more insurgents streamed in.

DeGrave called down to Colt and the others in the chamber, "Yo, take laptops, paperwork. Take everything—all that shit!"

While Sandlin, DeGrave, and others stormed the empty Senate, insurgents who were still trying to make their way into the building powered up the Capitol steps to the east entrance, pushing their way past the iconic Columbus Doors. Cutting through this unruly mob was a well-disciplined contingent of Oath Keepers ascending, single file, in a "stack" formation: each member's hand on the shoulder of the member ahead.

Some of the Oath Keepers had been providing backup security for VIPs such as Trump operative Roger Stone at the Willard Hotel the day before, as well as for Trump allies who spoke at the rally earlier on January 6th. Dressed in tactical military gear, the Oath Keepers communicated via a walkie-talkie app called Zello.

Among the ten or eleven Oath Keepers in the stack was US Army Ranger veteran Jessica Watkins, 38, of Ohio.

Soon after Trump lost the election, in a message to an associate, she expressed concern that militia members who wanted to help Trump assert his continuing claim to the presidency might get caught in an "elaborate trap."

"If Trump asks me to come, I will," she wrote, stating that the president had the right to "activate units," presumably meaning private militias. "Otherwise, I can't trust it."

While a president can use a state's "militia" to suppress a rebellion under the Insurrection Act, that's normally interpreted to mean the National Guard, not private militias. But Oath Keepers' founder Stewart Rhodes, a Yale-educated former prosecutor, had written, in an open letter, that Trump, if he invoked the Act, would have the right to call up ordinary citizens as a militia to "stop the steal." This appeared to be the interpretation Watkins was relying upon. Trump's incessant calls to "be there" on January 6th, apparently persuaded her that Trump might be ready to use this presumed power to legitimately "activate units" like the Oath Keepers.

And so, in late December 2020, she asked Donovan Crowl, another Oath Keeper, to join her on January 6th in Washington, DC, because "Trump wants all able-bodied patriots to come."

Coordinating with Watkins and Crowl was Thomas Caldwell, 65, of Virginia, who had held a top secret security clearance for decades, and had, for a time, worked for the FBI. Caldwell assigned himself the role of assembling heavy weapons and a "quick reaction force," to bring those munitions across the Potomac by boat, if needed.

Yet, it's not clear that they intended to use those munitions to storm the Capitol, or that an invasion of the building was part of the Oath Keepers' plan at all. Rhodes had warned that he did not trust the Pentagon or the defense secretary to ward off a "Benghazi-style attack" against Trump, presumably by antifa or some Deep State force. Defending against such an attack, he'd intimated, would be the Oath Keepers' job, along with serving as a militia should the president invoke the Insurrection Act.

Part of the plan or not, Watkins and her comrades got swept up in the mob mentality.

As the Oath Keepers left the Ellipse after Trump's speech ended, about thirty minutes prior to their "stack" climbing the steps, a male voice told those listening on the Zello app channel: "You are executing a citizen's arrest. Arrest this assembly, we have probable cause for acts of treason, election fraud."

If Watkins or anyone on the app channel had any argument with that directive, none expressed it.

Still, looking at her history, Jessica Watkins appeared, on the surface, to be the unlikeliest of Trump supporters. Enlisting in the US Army soon after graduating high school, in April 2001, Watkins was forced out in December 2003, less than two and one-half years later. Jeremy David was the name under which Watkins, the soldier, served. In 2004, she legally changed her name to Jessica Marie to match the gender she identified with.

She voted for Obama when he ran for president, the man who would reverse Don't Ask, Don't Tell, the Clinton-era policy that ended her army career.

Though she was no longer a soldier, the military was still in her blood. In 2019, she founded a tiny paramilitary group, the Ohio State Regular

Militia, to assist with first aid and security after tornadoes ripped through the city of Dayton, Ohio. Watkins acted as its commanding officer. But she made a point of stating that her group would not permit intolerance or extremism.

Trump had, meanwhile, reversed the Obama-era decision that had allowed transgender people to enlist in the military. Without calling it that, he had effectively brought back Don't Ask, Don't Tell for trans troops.

So, it might seem odd that Jessica Watkins would become such a fervent Trump supporter, especially since many if not most of the extremist groups that formed the foundation of Trump support were not just racist and misogynist; they were openly hostile to transgender people. Potentially violently so.

But we can't always presume someone's politics on the basis of the most prominent feature of the person's identity. On the cusp of World War II, one of Hitler's most effective spies in New York City was an Austrian-Jewish woman named Lilly Stein. She seduced men familiar with aspects of the United States' industrial and banking activities and relayed what they told her about war preparations to her German handlers.

Supreme Court Justice Clarence Thomas, though black, is the only member of the court to have openly questioned whether desegregating schools was, in and of itself, a good thing.

Watkins' case is more evidence that society's fixation on identity politics can miss the ways in which individual circumstances change the game.

Watkins, together with her longtime boyfriend, was a bar owner in the tiny rural town of Woodstock, Ohio. This small business, that she'd had such high hopes for, had been struggling due to restrictions imposed by the state government to decrease the spread of Covid-19. She didn't blame the virus. She blamed Republican Governor

Mike DeWine, the man who declared an emergency in March 2020 in an attempt to contain the virus's spread. DeWine's order that closed bars and restaurants to indoor customers was lifted in late May 2020. But business still lagged. And during the idle hours imposed by the pandemic, Watkins developed a penchant for watching videos produced by the conspiracy site, InfoWars.

Trump, meanwhile, was downplaying Covid-19's risks and constantly pushing to re-open the economy. He must have seemed to be on the side of businesses like hers.

After seeing Stewart Rhodes, Oath Keepers' founder, on one of InfoWars' segments, Watkins joined up and allied her militia with Rhodes's group. She and her boyfriend answered Rhodes's call to travel to Louisville, Kentucky, to help "maintain order," when protests escalated to violence and vandalism over the killing of Breonna Taylor.

Steeped in InfoWars conspiracy theories, and feeling, after witnessing the chaos that followed police shootings of black people, that the country was falling apart, Watkins probably didn't have to take much of a leap to believe Trump's Big Lie. About the only conspiracy that InfoWars' host, Alex Jones, failed to embrace was the one unfolding in plain sight: Trump's attempt at a self-coup.

As early as November, Watkins appeared to have been awaiting the orders she imagined Trump would be giving to private militias in his quest to take back the presidency from the man she viewed as a usurper. Each step brought her closer to disaster.

As formidable as the Oath Keepers, in tactics and rhetoric, might have appeared to outsiders, once inside the Capitol, they seemed less a fearsome fighting unit than a group of military cosplayers who were in over their heads. They took video selfies in the Rotunda, congratulated each other for taking over the building, and hooted it up as if their sports team had just scored the winning goal. They then streamed into a narrow hallway with the rest of the mob, intent on making their way to the Senate.

But cops in riot gear blocked the end of the passageway, preventing the tightly packed throng from advancing. Watkins admonished those in front of her in the hallway to "Push, push, *push*...Get in there. They can't hold us!"

She was wrong. They could hold the line, and they did. Police tossed tear gas into the crowd. The mob backed away. At just past three o'clock, the defeated Oath Keepers, including Watkins, retreated from the building.

Among those Oath Keepers still outside the building, some insisted on their chat app that any bad acts had to be the work of antifa infiltrators.

The couple dozen rioters who did make it to the Senate chamber found it eerily quiet—except, of course, for the strange, animal-like noises coming from the gallery, above. There, mugging for a videographer, was Jacob Chansley, the ubiquitous QAnon Shaman, pounding his spear rhythmically on the floor as he chanted something that sounded like, "Ay-ay-oh-ah. Ay-ay-oh-ah. Ay-ay-oh-ah. *YAAAAAAAAA!*"

On the Senate floor, most ignored him as they milled about, some rifling through the hinged desks of the senators. A husky man in a beige Henley shirt angrily flipped pages in a senator's loose-leaf binder, saying, "There's gotta be something we can fucking use against these scumbags," as others gathered around. Some took photos with their phones of the documents they found. Some just took the documents.

They soon came upon the desk used by Ted Cruz. Skimming his Arizona certification objection speech, they reassured each other that there were doing what Cruz would want them to do.

The time was 2:55 pm and the QAnon Shaman had begun a new wordless chant when a southern-accented voice yelled up at him to,

"Quit actin' a fool."

A lean young man in a MAGA hat made himself comfortable in the presiding officer's chair on the dais, declaring Trump, "Emperor of the United States." A heavyset man carrying zip-tie handcuffs and wearing tactical military gear—green helmet, green body armor—demanded, "Get outta that chair." They couldn't be disrespectful, he insisted. They were in a PR (public relations) war. At the same time, the man with the southern accent scolded the chair-sitter about his emperor comment: "We're a democracy."

The man holding the zip-tie handcuffs was retired Lieutenant Colonel Larry Brock, 53, of Texas, a former Air Force fighter pilot. The fellow with the southern accent was Joshua Black, 44, of Alabama, slender, bearded, wearing an over-sized camouflage jacket, and a red MAGA hat. Bloody after being shot in the lower left cheek with a rubber bullet, Black appeared unperturbed by his wound.

Both Brock and Black had called for the overthrow of the government. Black believed he had been led by God to join in a second American revolution. Brock had posted a message online for men with guns to shoot their way into the Capitol.

But, at that moment, these two cooled the overheated dynamic in the chamber. Where, minutes before, Nathan DeGrave had yelled at his fellow rioters to steal everything they could get their hands on, Brock and Black insisted that those around them show some respect for the "sacred" place they occupied. Though both members of the mob, and potentially violent themselves, they were nevertheless, the adults in the room. And those tempted toward havoc reluctantly listened when they calmly insisted on order.

Meanwhile, no longer getting the attention he craved in the now empty gallery, Chansley, the QAnon Shaman, carrying a bullhorn and his ever-present spear, entered the chamber through a pair of French doors at the back of the chamber and strutted toward the front. A cop trailed in about ten feet behind him.

Officer Robishaw, red-haired, wearing a blue surgical mask, and an ordinary patrol uniform with no protective gear, was one of those who had been among Officer Goodman's backup when they corralled Doug Jensen's group of insurrectionists almost an hour earlier. Now, Robishaw was alone. He approached with the cautious demeanor of a hostage negotiator—apparently aware that, at any moment, he could become the hostage.

Black, sitting on the floor, leaning against the front of the marble dais, was talking on his cell phone. The cop, noticing his injury, asked if he needed medical attention. Black demurred, then explained to the person he was speaking to on the phone that he'd been shot in the face.

In a calm, almost soothing tone, Robishaw asked those milling around the chamber: "Any chance I could get you guys to leave the Senate wing?"

"We will," Black responded. "I been makin' sure they ain't disrepectin' the place."

But QAnon Shaman Chansley wasn't ready to go. He ambled up to the dais, called Pence a "fucking traitor," and asked one of the others in the chamber to take a photo of him as he posed. Then he scribbled an all-caps note for Pence:

"IT'S ONLY A MATTER OF TIME. JUSTICE IS COMING!"

Officer Robishaw again calmly asked them to leave. Chansley, instead, began leading the group in a disjointed prayer. He rambled on, thanking God for "filling this chamber with patriots," and for allowing them to "get rid of the communists, the globalists, and the traitors within our government."

By the time Chansley finished, at about 3:15 pm, with a shouted, "Amen," police back-up had arrived. But the couple dozen insurrectionists left in the chamber showed none of the aggression toward these officers that had been on display in earlier fierce tussles with cops.

Instead, the riot seemed to have fizzled out of these rioters. Peacefully accepting an escort to the outside, some thanked the officers as they exited.

"We support you guys," an insurrectionist in a yellow plaid shirt called out to the police as he walked down the hall toward the exit. "We know you're doing your job."

At 3:04 pm, acting Defense Secretary Christopher Miller agreed to order the "activation" of the entire one-thousand-one-hundred troops of the DC National Guard. Between 3:19 pm and 3:26 pm, Army Secretary McCarthy informed Senate Majority Leader Charles Schumer, Speaker of the House Nancy Pelosi, DC Mayor Muriel Bowser, and MPD Police Chief Contee of Miller's decision.

But Miller's order was far less than it first appeared to be.

An order to "activate" or to "mobilize" the National Guard wasn't the same as an order to "deploy" the National Guard. All that Miller's activation order did was to tell those serving in the DC National Guard that it was time to leave their homes, head to the armory, and await orders—assuming such orders would come.

As it turned out, no orders would be coming any time soon. With the Capitol overrun, the vice president hiding with his family and staff in the basement, lawmakers packed tightly together in a secure location—and some, barricaded in their offices—Miller still hadn't agreed to take that necessary last step: to deploy the National Guard.

Meanwhile, General Walker, the DC National Guard's commander, assuming the order to deploy would come at any moment, directed the one-hundred-fifty Guard troops in his Quick Reaction Force to leave Andrews Air Force Base in Maryland, for the DC Armory, from which they could then deploy to the Capitol, once orders arrived. Walker arranged a police escort for the Quick Reaction Force, so there would be not a moment's delay.

MEANWHILE, IN THE SENATE

They reached the armory in about twenty minutes. And there they sat, waiting.

They were ready to go. But Miller, Trump's hand-picked post-election defense secretary, wasn't ready to deploy. He continued to slow-walk the process.

6

Last Stand on the Lower West Terrace

"A crowd that professes their love for law enforcement assaulted those police officers, dragged them, sprayed them, stomped on them."

— President Joe Biden, January 6, 2022, commemorating the first anniversary of the insurrection

O fficer Daniel Hodges couldn't rest for more than a few moments after escaping from insurrectionists who'd attacked him and tried to gouge out his eye.

If Hodges realized he needed medical help, he didn't make it his priority. The Capitol grounds had become a hellscape of MAGA-attired men and women.

Leaving the relative safety of a hallway where he'd temporarily retreated, he answered the call for reinforcements at the lower west terrace tunnel.

Cries and shouts of combat rising from behind the double doors down the corridor ahead guided him to where he was needed. Smoke and chemical residue fogged the air but the full gas mask he wore protected his lungs and his eyes. Fellow officers were just inside the entrance, an open arched tunnel that the president-elect would walk through in two weeks' time at his inauguration—provided police could hold the Capitol today against those determined to thwart the transfer of power.

Officers were stacked six or seven across and deep, shields up, somehow holding back the insurgents who had already smashed the glass of the first set of double doors leading into the building. They doused the officers at the front line with bear spray and other chemical sprays, and battered them with sticks, bats, feet, and fists. Hodges and other newer arrivals filled gaps in the back of the line.

His radio gone in the earlier battle, and radio communications sparse to non-existent anyway, Hodges and others in the tunnel didn't realize that parts of the mob had gained entry through other doors and windows. As far as the cops guarding the tunnel knew, this was the last line of defense. In a way, they were right. Other law enforcement had begun to clear those who'd gotten inside. But if Hodges and his fellow officers failed to hold back the hordes bent on breaking through their line, thousands more would surge through the building. It was anyone's guess what a mob that viciously attacked and overwhelmed a line of cops would do to the trapped vice president and lawmakers if they made it through.

"We've got to hold this door!" shouted the MPD commander.

Just several dozen officers against thousands—not great odds—but they were determined to follow that order, even if it killed them.

It very nearly would.

California native Danny Rodriguez, 38, was like a great many others who showed up in Washington, DC, on January 6, 2021. He felt great reverence for the idea of the US Constitution, but had only a vague understanding of what was in it, and an equally hazy grasp of how his government actually worked. Much of what Rodriguez believed about both came from programming on the web, particularly InfoWars. What he learned there was demonstrably wrong. But he didn't know that. He trusted host Alex Jones, Jones's guests, and other YouTube personalities when they claimed to reveal the hidden "truths" that traditional television and print media didn't want their audiences to know.

A fan of Donald Trump's since his reality TV series, *The Apprentice*, Rodriguez felt like he knew the man, and thought of Trump almost as if he were an old friend. When Trump first ran for president in 2016, Rodriguez volunteered to make calls and canvass for him, door-to-door. He attended anti-Trump protests, too, but only to defend his candidate, sometimes arguing with Trump haters for hours, trying to get them to see the truth as he understood it.

Though he didn't consider himself a member of QAnon, Rodriguez did believe that Trump was battling a cabal of evil, elite pedophiles. That story had been circulating before Q first appeared. Rodriguez saw no reason to doubt it.

He also accepted, without question, that the election had been stolen from Trump. His favorite YouTube channel personalities claimed to have irrefutable evidence of an anti-Trump plot. And Covid-19 was part of it. As Rodriguez understood it, the virus had been designed more to kill the economy than to kill people. But even though he knew the pandemic had hurt Trump, he still couldn't believe Trump had lost. He didn't buy that for a minute, but he did worry that the people who stole the election planned to round up Trump supporters like himself.

He decided he had to act. He'd learned from internet sources that the first American revolution, in 1776, was fought and won by just three-percent of the population. If just three-percent could take down a corrupt government then, couldn't three-percent do it now?

Days before the January 6th Save America rally, along with a half dozen other Trump supporters, Rodriguez piled into a rented van headed for Washington, DC, determined to be one of the good guys who would help stop the steal.

He watched Trump's speech at the Ellipse, then joined the crowd to march on the Capitol. With thousands of fellow Trump supporters, he got all the way up to the building itself. There, chaos reigned. Patriots were singing songs. Waving flags. It was madness but it was enthralling. He climbed the scaffolding, looked around, and soaked in the thrill of all that was happening around him, everyone who was there, like him, to save America. As he descended, he saw a thousand or more patriots converging on one spot, an opening in the building. A tunnel. He made his way toward it.

Like MPD Officer Daniel Hodges, Capitol Police Sergeant Aquilino Gonell, 43, raced to the lower west terrace tunnel to help reinforce the wall of cops holding back the rampaging mob. He was stunned by their ferocity. Some insurgents had come armed, prepared to attack cops like him with bear spray, hammers, rebars, knives, and flagpoles sharpened into spears. Those who hadn't carried in their own weapons broke apart the bike rack barricades and turned the pieces into improvised bludgeons, or stole police batons and riot shields to use against them.

Gonell had fought in Iraq. This was more terrifying than anything he'd encountered there: a medieval battle that pitted a handful of men and women in uniform against a berserk, rabid mob, surging toward them in waves, fresh fighters taking up the attack at the mouth of the tunnel as earlier combatants, spent, fell back.

But even in the midst of the melee, Gonell could see that a few insurgents were coordinating their efforts with each other. They used hand signals to alert each other or communicated through earpieces.

They clearly had a plan. Gonnell figured these pockets of collaborators had to have had military or law enforcement training.

As one of the few officers who still had his shield, he positioned himself at the front of the line. Rioters shouted threats against Speaker Pelosi and Vice President Pence, and called the officers traitors to the very Constitution that Gonell and his brothers and sisters in uniform were defending against this relentless attack.

Above the din, he heard a scream of agony. It came from somewhere close, within the line of officers. The sound chilled him. He wanted to break from formation to help, but his discipline said no: doing so without someone to take his place could mean allowing legions of subversives to pour through the resulting breach.

He held his position.

Officer Daniel Hodges had moved up to the front, adding his shield to those of fellow officers with whom he stood shoulder-to-shoulder. They fought to control just a few feet of tunnel, sometimes mere inches. But every inch counted.

Hodges felt sure that if they could just hold the line a little while longer, reinforcements would arrive. Some of the most powerful people in the world were trapped in that building.

In fact, some reinforcements were already trickling in from the FBI and nearby police jurisdictions. But the DC National Guard had not yet even been authorized.

A military veteran himself, it would not have occurred to Hodges that acting Defense Secretary Christopher Miller would be dragging his feet, resisting the pleas to deploy, while this brutal battle streamed live across the country and the world.

Insurgents had been yanking shields from hands of the cops and passing them back to other rioters. A heavyset, sixty-ish bald man who had already stolen at least one police shield grabbed for another. A cop at the front line warned him: release it or be sprayed. The man refused, then collapsed, complaining of asthma, as a stream of chemical gas forced him to loosen his grip.

Some officers pulled the stricken man inside and administered first aid. The front line moved forward, gaining a bit of ground against the mob. Hodges, now face-to-face with the insurrectionists, braced himself against a metal doorframe halfway down the tunnel entrance to help him hold his position. One of the few who still had his gas mask, shield, and baton, he was ready for them.

Without warning, the momentum shifted. The cops got pushed back, losing the ground they'd just gained. Insurrectionists, at least fifty deep outside and at the mouth of the tunnel, moved against them as one.

"Heave-*ho*! Heave-*ho*!"

Hodges, still wedged between the door and its metal frame, got caught in this wave and found himself unable to move in any direction. "*Heave-ho!*"

The mob surged again. "Heave-*ho!*"

To his left, a rioter took advantage of his vulnerability and slammed a shield against him. With all the weight of all the bodies behind him, pushing from the mouth of the tunnel, he had Hodges trapped between the shield on his left and the doorframe to his right.

Arms pinned, Hodges cried for help.

Another insurgent, seeing Hodges immobilized, grabbed his gas mask, and used it to bash Hodges' head against the door. Blow after dizzying blow told the trapped officer: these might be his last moments.

The man, trying to yank Hodges' mask entirely off his face, succeeded only in stretching the strap against Hodges' neck, increasing the cop's agony. Hodges struggled to free his arms while his attacker practically foamed at the mouth, wordlessly screaming in rage or glee—Hodges couldn't tell which.

As the insurgent at last stripped the mask off his face, Hodges gulped in a rush of chemical spray.

"Heave-*ho!*" The mob pressed forward, forcing the air from his lungs.

Someone grabbed the baton from Hodges' immobilized hand and began pummeling him with it—smashing it against his skull, his shoulders, his face. His lip ruptured.

All he could do was scream.

At last, another officer was able to help Hodges dislodge himself, and pulled the badly injured cop to the rear. A few feet away, at the front line, Sergeant Aquilino Gonell battled on in hand-to-hand combat with flag-draped lunatics who hollered gleefully that Trump had sent them.

A rioter cracked a baton against Gonnell's hand, adding to multiple traumas his body had already suffered. The pain registered, but adrenaline and survival instincts pushed it to the back of his mind. Gonell was realistic about their chances—not good— but for as long as he was able, he was going to keep them from crossing the line.

The mob grabbed an officer near him, attempting to yank him out of the tunnel. Gonnell grasped the back of the officer's collar and pulled him back to the police line. A moment later, they almost got another. As Gonnell reached out to help this second officer, he stepped on a pile of riot shields, slick with pepper and bear spray. He slipped, lost his footing, and fell hard. The mob immediately descended, taking advantage of Gonnell's sudden vulnerability. Hostile hands grabbed his leg, tugged his riot shield, dragged him forward by his shoulder strap. His shoulder felt like it was being wrenched out of its socket.

He fought back with equal ferocity, punching, kicking, clawing in a desperate attempt to right himself. He looked to nearby officers for aid but they were also under attack. If anyone was going to save him, it would be he, himself. The blows piled injury on injury, but somehow, he bested them, using his own baton to thwart an insurgent who was bent on dragging him into the mob. Finally able to right himself, Gonell fell back in line, his body broken in a half dozen ways.

With no relief in sight, he fought on.

If Central Casting were to choose someone to play the quintessential Irish beat cop of a bygone time, he would look very much like Jimmy Albright—red-haired, earnest, reassuringly solid—the kind of officer who could make a neighborhood street feel safer just by his presence.

At the other end of the cop spectrum, Michael Fanone exuded a daredevil vibe. Wiry, intense, tattooed from wrists to neck, he'd spent much of his police career undercover, rubbing elbows with criminals.

Superficial differences aside, after working together in DC's Metropolitan Police Department for about five years, the two were the best of buddies. And each felt a kinship bond with others in law enforcement.

Distress calls had been coming from the Capitol Police while Fanone was on his way to a buy-and-bust operation in DC. Through radio transmissions, he learned that MPD officers who had been deployed initially to help the Capitol Police hold back the rioters had run out of less-lethal weapons like tear gas and chemical spray. There was nothing left at the station, either. Their situation dire, they were calling for volunteers from the MPD, and help from neighboring jurisdictions.

The undercover op would have to happen another day. Fanone turned around and headed for the station. There, he met up with Albright, who had just begun changing into his uniform so he, too, could self-deploy to the Capitol. They grabbed the necessary tactical gear: vests, body-worn cameras, radios, helmets, and gas masks. Fanone reached into his locker for the blue uniform that had hung there for years. As a plain clothesman, he'd never before worn it. Tearing off its plastic wrapping, he suited up.

They grabbed the keys for a police car from a sergeant in the parking lot for the short trip to the Capitol, with Albright driving, arriving at 3:04 pm, parking outside the Longworth Building, one of several structures where congressional representatives had offices and conducted meetings. The street was lined with dozens of empty white police cars and vans. The sidewalks, usually bustling on a weekday afternoon, were deserted. All the action was centered on the Capitol building, itself.

Albright and Fanone wore the ubiquitous surgical masks of the pandemic but left their gas masks in the car. As they made their way toward the building, distress calls dominated radio transmissions: *officer down... officer needs assistance.* Albright noticed a trail of blood on the ground.

They entered via the southeast entrance into a corridor lined with massive fluted white pillars that, in better times, evinced dignified serenity. From there, they walked down toward the lower west terrace, where the most urgent calls for help arose, passing scattered law enforcement in blue and camouflage uniforms, some of whom had come from different jurisdictions to reinforce the Capitol Police.

One floor down, outside a pair of double doors that led to the tunnel, they encountered a number of officers who had been at the front line, including a long-time friend and colleague of Fanone's, Commander Ramey Kyle. The eyes of all these cops had been so drenched with tear gas and pepper spray, they were little more than swollen red slits. The officers passed bottled water from one to another, washing as much of the toxic residue from their faces as they could before they headed back into the fray.

Fanone and Albright fell in line behind them.

A chemical fog wafted around their ankles as they made their way forward across a floor slimed by what other cops, overcome by chemical sprays, had chucked up. Forty or fifty exhausted officers had been battling for control of this entrance for the better part of an hour. Some wore full protective gear—gas masks, helmets, body armor. Others were bare-faced, lacking shields, and fully exposed. A number were visibly hurt, some bloody.

"We need to get some fresh bodies up there," called Fanone.

Echoing him, Albright hollered, "Let's get some fresh guys up front." On the other side of the tunnel, a new chant rose from the mob: *"Pull the cops out. Pull the cops out. Pull the cops out. Pull the cops out."*

Just minutes earlier, the insurrectionists had almost succeeded in capturing Sergeant Aquilino Gonnell and a couple of other officers. Gonnell had inhaled and swallowed more chemical spray than seemed possible, and was having trouble breathing. He heard a voice shout, "Come on, guys, I just got here. Back up if you need a break."

He didn't know the voice but he knew he needed that break if he was going to be any good to anyone ever again. Gonnell backed up.

Mike Fanone took his place at the front line. Albright, to his left and inches behind him, held Fanone's vest so they wouldn't be separated.

Having entered from the east side of the building, they'd never glimpsed the legions of MAGA-hatted, flag-draped, brawlers who had been battling their brothers and sisters in blue at the entrance to the west terrace tunnel. They looked out at the hordes of insurgents, many armed with sticks, bats, hammers, crutches, stolen police riot shields, flagpoles sharpened into spears, and realized, for the first time, what they were up against. This was a battle right out of the Dark Ages. Just one small point was in their favor: despite being insanely outnumbered, only so many of the mob could push into the narrow space of the tunnel at any one time. It didn't make it a fair fight but it might be winnable, if they could push them back far enough, and close the double doors a few yards inside the mouth of the tunnel. If they failed to hold the line, the mob wouldn't just overrun the building, free to attack whoever they encountered. Every cop in that tunnel would be trampled.

"Back it up!" Fanone yelled, pushing at the rioters.

"Give us the right people," one yelled back. Translation: give us Pence, Pelosi, and others on Trump's enemies' list.

Ignoring the taunt, Fanone focused on getting the doors closed.

An insurgent with a stolen police shield thrust it forward and countless others added their weight to his in a rush to get through the doors and deeper inside.

"Heave-ho. Heave-ho."

"Come on, MPD, push these motherfuckers back," Fanone shouted, as much to psych himself as to anyone else. "Dig in. Push them back. C'*mon* MPD!"

The time was about 3:15 pm and chaos reigned. But there was something markedly different about the insurrectionists who had made it to the front of the battle line and their thousands of compatriots who hung back, cheering them on.

Those at the front had tasted blood and wanted more. The battering of fists, feet, flagpoles, and other improvised weapons against police flesh turned this contingent of otherwise ordinary people into animalistic combatants. Some were clearly ready to fight to the death, if it came to that, abandoning all rational thought, drunk on their own adrenaline.

But against the odds, the cops managed to gain ground, first a couple of yards, then further still. Invigorated by their momentum, the officers kept pushing, all the way to the threshold.

Then one of the cops hollered, "Knife!"

Albright saw it, too: black, with a six-inch long blade. He quickly slapped it out of the insurrectionist's hand, grabbed it from the ground where it dropped, and passed it back over his shoulder to the officers behind him. In the seconds it took to do that, Fanone, who had been mere inches from him since they got there, was gone.

"I got one!" shouted a voice from the mob.

They got one, Danny Rodriguez saw. His fellow Trump supporters, patriots as they styled themselves, were yanking a man out of the tunnel. At first, he thought they were wrestling with another patriot. But no, they'd snared one of the cops blocking them from getting inside to stop the steal.

They dragged the cop on his stomach down the steps, away from the tunnel entrance, and into the mob. The officer struggled mightily but too many hands held him for him to escape. One hit him with a crutch, another with a baton. A third bludgeoned him with a flagpole attached to the thin blue line flag that patriots waved to show their respect for police.

Rodriguez held a taser in his hand.

Like others in the crowd, he backed the blue. He considered himself a loyal ally of the police, the good ones who, in his eyes, were fighting against the forces of antifa and BLM.

But this officer was on the wrong side. He was protecting the evil people inside that building—pedophiles who stole elections, who would destroy the country if no one stopped them.

Rodriguez was there to stop them, to be a hero.

He reached out with his taser, pressed it to the cop's neck, and pulled the trigger.

The cop screamed in agony.

He tased him again.

It all happened so quickly, Fanone couldn't say who dragged him from the tunnel or how. Single-minded as a hydra, the mob came at him from every direction, a mad raging monster with dozens of limbs. That monster meant to kill him.

"Get his gun."

"Kill him with his own gun."

Hands grasped his radio, stripped away his ammunition belt, tore the badge from his vest. Powerless against them or the metal weapons they used to beat his torso, his arms, his legs, he struggled to escape.

Someone lunged for his gun. Fanone managed to hang onto it, thinking fleetingly that he could try to shoot his way out. Bad idea, he realized. He might get a couple of them, but then they'd kill him for sure.

Then, beyond any torture he could have imagined, came the jolt of electrocution to his neck. Waves of liquid lightning charged through his body, lighting up every nerve ending, screeching through his veins, his muscles, his viscera.

He was going to die here.

He thought of his four daughters. He would never see them again. What would they do without their dad?

Close to losing consciousness, he had one hope left: if he could reach just a couple of them—appeal to their humanity.

"I got kids," he cried out.

Jimmy Albright looked down into the mob and saw an insurrectionist dragging Fanone back up toward him at the tunnel entrance. He reached out to grab his partner, pulled him back behind him and into the arms of other officers, then turned to the mob to make sure no one was following behind.

One of the cops carrying Fanone called for an EMT.

"I got it," Albright shouted. "He's my partner."

Pulling him into a corner in the corridor, Albright cradled the limp, unconscious Fanone. He wasn't sure at first that he was even alive.

"Mike, stay in there, buddy. Mike, it's Jimmy, I'm here, Mike."

He was alive. Albright could see that now. But he wasn't responding and he seemed to be having trouble breathing.

"You've gotta hold on, man... Mike, I'm here for you, buddy. C'mon dude. Come on buddy...."

Had he lost him? He kept talking, kept trying to reach Fanone in those deep recesses of the unconscious that his friend had disappeared into, telling him he needed him to wake up. They had plans. They were going to go duck hunting together—remember?

"C'mon, Mike."

Could he hear him?

Minutes ticked by. Finally, Fanone stirred, back to the world of the living.

Weakly, he looked up at Albright. "Did you take that door back?"

Relieved beyond imagining, Albright told him, yes.

"We took the fucking door back."

The mob, meanwhile, had pulled another officer into its midst, savaging him as they had Fanone, but all Albright could focus on at that moment was getting his friend to a hospital. Bruised and beaten himself, and dizzy from the chemicals the rioters sprayed at them, he did his best to support Fanone, his arm around his shoulder, as they made their way back to the vehicle they'd left near the Longworth building less than an hour before. On the way, Albright had to stop to heave up some of the chemicals he'd been forced to inhale and swallow.

As Albright drove him to the emergency room, Fanone fell in and out of consciousness. Albright half-carried him to the ER's reception desk, pushing past a guard concerned that they weren't wearing masks.

The ER waiting room was packed. Injured police lay on gurneys or sat in chairs, waiting for medical attention next to some of the same insurrectionists who had inflicted their injuries.

An attendant asked for Fanone's insurance information. Before he could hand it over, he collapsed again.

At 4:17 pm, Trump, at long last, told those who had stormed the Capitol on his behalf to end the siege.

123

"I know your pain. I know you're hurt. We had an election that was stolen from us. It was a landslide election, and everyone knows it, especially the other side, but you have to go home now..."

Trump ended his video by saying he loved the insurrectionists and called them "very special" before reiterating that it was time for them to go home.

One minute later, at 4:18 pm, acting Defense Secretary Miller gave the order to mobilize National Guard troops from nearby states, although he did not yet permit the deployment of the DC Guard, standing at the ready in a nearby armory, awaiting orders.

QAnon Shaman Jacob Chansley, shouted out to those around him, "Trump said to go home." Having run with what he believed were Trump's orders to invade the Capitol, he and hundreds of others now followed Trump's order to retreat.

Soldiers use a term, "fog of war," to explain how communications and other issues break down in battle. For a great many of those who had been pounding at the cops holding them back from getting inside through the tunnel, an order from the man they came to fight for wasn't enough to get them to lay down their weapons. By that point, Trump's "go home" message was like telling sharks in a feeding frenzy that lunch hour was over, and expecting them to simply swim away.

They weren't having it.

Ryan Nichols wasn't having it. He who had once ventured into a hurricane to rescue trapped dogs, and won applause on Ellen DeGeneres's show, had spent the last half-hour or so in a Capitol conference room he'd reached through a broken arched window next to the tunnel. With a friend, he'd barricaded the door that would have led them further into the building. Though they'd dithered in the room for a while, Nichols was ready for more action. He positioned himself on a ledge near the tunnel entrance, turned to the mob, and shouted into his bullhorn.

"If you have a weapon, you need to get your weapon. This is the second revolution right here folks. This is not a peaceful protest."

The roaring voices of thousands mostly drowned him out. But his call to arms was superfluous. The mob knew what it was there to do. Stop the steal. Punish the vice president for disloyalty. Disrupt the counting of electoral votes. With or without Trump's blessing.

Some of the more violent insurrectionists were now facing off against the exhausted police. They included David Nicholas Dempsey, who had, earlier in the day, hollered threats next to the makeshift gallows that others had erected, and who now appeared ready to match deeds to words. Climbing on the backs and shoulders of fellow rioters, he pounded the officers at the front line with crutches and a metal pole, and sprayed them with chemicals. Another man bludgeoned cops with a broken wooden table leg. Someone sprayed them with a fire extinguisher then heaved the empty cylinder into the tunnel at them. Rioters clambered over other rioters, so eager for a chance to beat down the cops, they didn't seem to care what they did to those on their own side. It was madness squared.

A man near the entrance screamed that his friend was being trampled. Sergeant Aquilino Gonell rushed forward to help. He found Roseanne Boyland on the ground, unconscious.

Roseanne Boyland, 34, had never been much interested in politics, but she adored children, particularly her two nieces. She became convinced that the QAnon conspiracy theories were real, especially one that claimed that children were being trafficked in furniture shipped by the online retailer Wayfair. Somehow, that led her to seeing Trump as a savior of endangered children, and from there, it was easy to believe that she had to go to Washington, DC, to help stop the steal and thereby save the children from pedophiles. It didn't help that Boyland suffered from substance abuse and that pandemic restrictions on gatherings had cut her off from her AA meetings.

As Gonell and other officers tried to help Boyland, an insurrectionist reached over her limp body to attack them with a baton.

But Gonell managed to pull the woman into the tunnel, then past the inside corridor where injured officers were tending to their own wounds.

Meanwhile, increasingly blood-thirsty insurgents threw everything they had at the police still at the tunnel entrance.

One charged at an officer, grabbed him by the face, and knocked him off his feet. Another man grabbed the cop's baton, while a third pulled him by the head and helmet into the mob.

The assailant who stole the baton raced back to the entrance to yank a second officer into the mob, using the baton around the cop's neck to drag him, face-first, down the steps.

Surrounding their captives, the crazed assailants stomped cops with booted feet, battered them with flagpoles and crutches, ripped away their gas masks, and doused their exposed and battered faces with chemical spray.

Gonell saw none of this as he worked to get the unconscious woman to a safer place. Fellow Capitol Police officer, Harry Dunn, who had been clearing rioters out of the Rotunda, saw the injured Gonell struggling to carry the woman and hurried to assist. Dunn, a mountain of a man whose physique could terrify any adversary—but whose guileless smile immediately put people at ease—helped carry Boyland up the stairs.

The officers administered CPR but it was futile. Boyland was gone.

Gonell noted the time of death as 4:26 pm, then took the opportunity to call his family—the first chance he'd had that day to let them know he was still alive.

At 4:32 pm, acting Defense Secretary Miller finally approved deployment of the DC National Guard. DC National Guard Commander Walker was notified of the approval at 5:08 pm, and Guardsmen began arriving at the Capitol by 5:20 pm.

Fresh police reinforcements arrived from neighboring jurisdictions, armed with tear gas and other less lethal weapons, and began pushing back the last of the violent insurrectionists from the lower west terrace tunnel.

As dusk fell on the city, law enforcement and National Guard quickly cleared the remaining members of the mob from the Capitol and its grounds.

But still, more pain was to come.

As the officers who had battled insurgents through the afternoon washed chemicals from their eyes and skin, and tried to decompress, a call went out over the radio that a fellow officer had collapsed. That officer was Brian Sicknick. EMTs administered CPR on the floor of the Capitol building, but the hospital listed him in critical condition upon his arrival. He suffered two strokes in succession in the aftermath of fighting to save the Capitol. Officer Sicknick died the following day, January 7, 2021. He was 42 years old.

7

Aftermath

"Mr. Trump ignored the rulings of the courts and launched a massive campaign to mislead the public. Our hearings will show that these falsehoods provoked the violence on Jan. 6."

— **Congresswoman Liz Cheney, writing in the *Wall Street Journal*, February 2022**

B y 6:30 pm, the last of the insurrectionists had been cleared from the Capitol building and grounds. Key lawmakers, including House Speaker Nancy Pelosi and Senate Majority Leader Mitch McConnell, who had been taken to Fort McNair, a nearby army base, to keep them safe during the insurrection, returned to the Capitol soon after.

Vice President Mike Pence and his family never left the building throughout the siege. For almost five hours, beneath the Senate wing, they had sheltered in a barren concrete underground garage's loading dock—no windows or furniture—guarded by Secret Service agents.

At 8:06 pm, Pence was back on the Senate dais. His words were, "Let's get back to work," but the look on his face, as he called the Senate back into session, communicated something closer to, "Enough of this crap."

Senators and staff broke into applause. It seemed, in those first moments, that the country might pull together as one nation, regardless of party.

That hope was soon dashed.

On the House side, representatives were still filing in. Congresswoman Frederica Wilson (D-FL) had watched the insurrection in real-time on her television from her apartment just blocks from the Capitol and worried that there wouldn't be sufficient security to hold the vote that night. A police escort led her and a staffer back to the Capitol, where they assessed some of the damage before returning to participate in the count.

She saw streaks of blood on statues in Statuary Hall; other statues and ornaments had been broken and defaced. Several offices had been vandalized. Feces had been smeared along the floors and tracked through the building.

Before joining colleagues, she stopped at the ladies room near the Speaker's Lobby. Rioters had ripped the water cooler from the wall and smashed it. They had broken the mirrors, torn the sanitary napkin dispensers off the walls and scattered their contents over the floor.

Shaken by the evidence of so much rage and violence, Wilson quickly exited and took her seat in the House Chamber.

At 9:02 pm, Speaker Nancy Pelosi gaveled the House back to order.

Four hours of terror had little effect on the vote. One-hundred-thirty-eight Republican congressional representatives objected to the certification of Pennsylvania's electoral ballots; one-hundred-twenty-one Republican congressional representatives objected to certifying

Arizona's.

Congressman Greg Pence (R-IN), the vice president's brother, who had been evacuated with the rest of the Pence family minutes after insurrectionists first broke into the Capitol, voted against certifying Pennsylvania's electoral votes.

Five of the six congressman who assisted Capitol Police in barricading doors to the House chamber after insurgents tried to smash their way in—Markwayne Mullin (R-OK), Andrew Clyde (R-GA), Troy Nehls (R-TX), Pat Fallon (R-TX), and Ronny Jackson (R-TX)—objected to certifying the electoral ballots of both states. Months later, Congressman Clyde would be widely denounced for his attempt to re-write the history of that day, claiming—despite a photo that showed him grimacing or perhaps screaming in panic as insurrectionists tried to break down the door—that there was "no insurrection," that calling it one was a "bold-faced lie," and adding "if you didn't know the TV footage was a video from January the 6th, you would actually think it was a normal tourist visit."

In the Senate, seven Republicans, including Ted Cruz (R-TX), Josh Hawley (R-MO), and Rick Scott (R-FL) voted to object to Pennsylvania's ballots and six senators objected to Arizona's.

But when the grueling all-nighter ended at 3:42 am on the morning of January 7, 2021, Vice President Pence, in his capacity as president of the Senate, declared Joe Biden the winner of the 2020 presidential election.

Later on the afternoon of January 7th, Elaine Chao, Trump's transportation secretary, and the wife of Majority Leader Mitch McConnell, resigned, citing the siege of the Capitol. Education Secretary Betsy DeVos announced her resignation soon after Chao, for the same reasons. By Friday, January 8th, fourteen more Trump appointees, including six national security officials, had resigned over Trump's incitement of the insurrection.

House Speaker Pelosi and Senate Minority Leader Schumer feared what else the wounded, "unhinged," in Pelosi's estimation, and apparently desperate president might attempt in his bid to hang onto power during his final two weeks in office. The two Democratic leaders immediately called for Trump's removal via the 25ᵗʰ amendment. Invoking that amendment would have temporarily withdrawn Trump's presidential authority, making Mike Pence acting president. As long as Trump was still in charge, the country was at risk. Pelosi worried that Trump might even unilaterally decide to launch nuclear weapons at Iran or another perceived adversary. After what he'd already done since losing the election, almost anything seemed possible.

But only the vice president could invoke the 25ᵗʰ, along with at least half the cabinet. They would have to formally agree that Trump was "unable to discharge the powers and duties of his office."

Pence refused to consider such a move.

The next step was impeachment. The House passed a resolution stating that in the absence of Pence invoking the 25ᵗʰ amendment to remove Trump, members would proceed to impeach him. On January 13, 2021, the House did just that. All Democrats and ten Republicans voted in favor.

While House Minority Leader Kevin McCarthy (R-CA) acknowledged that Trump bore responsibility for the attack, and should have done something to stop it, he was reluctant to impeach, suggesting Trump should, instead, be censured.

Impeachment was only a first step, roughly equivalent to an indictment. To remove a president would require a vote to convict from at least two-thirds of the Senate, or sixty-seven senators.

Republican Senators, for the most part, despite having lived through the chaos of a Capitol under siege, balked at taking that final step.

At the end of Trump's impeachment trial, Senate Minority Leader Mitch McConnell (R-KY) condemned the former president with a withering rebuke, leaving no doubt that he held Trump responsible for spearheading an attempted coup d'état.

This was an intensifying crescendo of conspiracy theories, orchestrated by an outgoing president who seemed determined to either overturn the voters' decision or else torch our institutions on the way out.

The unconscionable behavior did not end when the violence began.

Whatever our ex-president claims he thought might happen that day, whatever reaction he says he meant to produce, by that afternoon, he was watching the same live television as the rest of the world.

A mob was assaulting the Capitol in his name. These criminals were carrying his banners, hanging his flags, and screaming their loyalty to him.

It was obvious that only President Trump could end this. Former aides publicly begged him to do so. Loyal allies frantically called the administration.

But the president did not act swiftly. He did not do his job. He didn't take steps so federal law could be faithfully executed, and order restored.

Instead, according to public reports, he watched television happily as the chaos unfolded. He kept pressing his scheme to overturn the election!

Even after it was clear to any reasonable observer that Vice President Pence was in danger, even as the mob carrying Trump banners was beating cops and breaching perimeters, the president sent a further tweet attacking his vice president.

Predictably and foreseeably under the circumstances, members of the mob seemed to interpret this as further inspiration to lawlessness and violence.

McConnell's speech followed his mind-boggling vote to acquit. He claimed that he didn't believe a former president could be convicted, since conviction meant removal and Trump was no longer in office. But conviction wasn't simply a tool to remove a sitting president. Conviction for having "engaged in insurrection... or giv[ing] aid or comfort" to those who did, would have barred Trump, under the fourteenth amendment to the Constitution, from ever holding federal office again.

In the end, just seven Republican senators voted to convict. Though they and all fifty Democratic senators constituted a 57 to 43 majority, it wasn't enough.

With nothing, to date, to impede him, after acquittal, Trump had a clear path to run again.

In the days following January 6th, long past the time when they were desperately needed, more than thirty-thousand National Guard troops were called to the Capitol from all fifty states and three territories. An eight-foot high metal fence topped with razor wire replaced the flimsy bike racks used as barricades on January 6th and stayed in place until March, when the belated reinforcements also began returning home.

Why the DC Guard wasn't immediately allowed to help drive out the insurrectionists is one of the enduring mysteries of January 6th.

On May 12, 2021, Congressman Hank Johnson (D-GA) attempted to get a clear explanation in his questioning of former acting Secretary of Defense Christopher Miller during a hearing before the House Committee on Oversight and Reform:

CONGRESSMAN HANK JOHNSON: *"So, in short, it was*

almost—it was three hours after the first request for National Guard assistance at the Capitol before permission was granted by you. Isn't that correct?"

FORMER ACTING DEFENSE SECRETARY CHRISTO-PHER MILLER: *"No, I don't think that's the case. A request—a 911 call does not equate to a formal request. I had an obligation."*

CONGRESSMAN JOHNSON: *"Well, let me ask you this. Did you—how did it come to pass that you slow-rolled the deployment of National Guard troops to put down a violent insurrection that you were observing taking place at the Capitol? How could it be—how could it be that three hours would pass before you authorized National Guard troops to reinforce the Capitol Hill police and the DC police?"*

Good question—and one that Miller never adequately answered, claiming that he ordered the full mobilization of the National Guard at 3:00 pm, without acknowledging that "full mobilization" wasn't, in fact, an order to deploy the Guard. His order simply put them on notice that a deployment order was likely to be forthcoming.

At best, Miller's response finessed the truth.

It took grilling by Congresswoman Alexandria Ocasio-Cortez (D-NY) and others to get Miller to admit during the Oversight Committee hearing that he failed to give the order to deploy despite numerous urgent requests to himself and Secretary of the Army Ryan McCarthy: from Mayor Bowser at 1:34 pm; from House Speaker Pelosi and Senate Minority Leader Schumer at 3:19 pm; and from Vice President Pence at 4:08 pm.

So, again, why the foot-dragging?

Without a window into Miller's thoughts at the time, all anyone can do is speculate.

Here's what we do know.

Major General William J. Walker, commanding general of the DC National Guard, in late-January 2021, said that all military commanders normally have authority to immediately respond to "protect property, life, and in my case, federal functions—federal property and life."

Just days before January 6th, Miller rescinded Walker's authority to respond to protect federal property and life without first getting both Miller's and Secretary of the Army Ryan McCarthy's explicit approval.

Because of this unusual restriction, Walker could not come to the aid of the Capitol Police without disobeying orders.

Miller, in his prepared testimony, before taking questions from Congressman Johnson and others, suggested that the use of overwhelming force against mostly peaceful Black Lives Matter protesters the previous summer had taught him a valuable lesson about the need for restraint.

But there's considerable difference between acting too aggressively against a peaceful protest, and not acting at all to stop a violent insurrection.

The timing of Miller's deployment orders also seemed a tad too synchronized with Trump's actions. Miller's first, to muster out-of-state National Guard, came exactly one minute after Trump posted his "go home... we love you." video message on Twitter.

Miller's verbal order to deploy the DC National Guard, which had been ready for hours to help clear the Capitol of insurrectionists, came fifteen minutes after Trump's Twitter video.

Six times during his testimony, Miller's excuse for slow-walking the Guard was that they should only be used as a "last resort."

Capitol Police were overwhelmed when the barricades were first breached. Numerous officials made urgent calls for the National Guard. Though reinforcements quickly arrived from MPD, they weren't enough to ensure the safety of those trapped inside though, miraculously, neither lawmakers nor the vice president were harmed.

The grossly outnumbered police were able to keep all of those under their protection in the Capitol safe, but that, in large part, was thanks to luck.

Pure luck.

Pence was still in his unsecured office near the Senate chamber, with insurrectionists storming through a mere hundred feet away, when Trump tweeted that his VP lacked the courage to "protect the Country and our Constitution."

A violent part of the mob, determined to chase down escaping congressional representatives, smashed the windowed doors leading to the Speaker's Lobby next to the House chamber. Had a Capitol Police officer not thwarted that pursuit by shooting Ashli Babbitt, how many lawmakers would they have taken down?

What, exactly, would a "last resort" look like, if not the above?

A couple of clues about what might have caused Miller to hesitate actually put him in a better light than his own testimony. Those clues have little to do with the over-the-top federal response to Black Lives Matter demonstrators six months earlier— or any of the other excuses offered for the delay.

Miller testified that when he met with Trump on January 3rd, the then-president asked if there were any requests for the National Guard. Miller told him that Mayor Bowser had made such a request. Trump then told him to "fill it and do whatever was necessary to protect the demonstrators."

The comment about using the Guard to protect pro-Trump demonstrators came up for further scrutiny when, months later, the House Select Committee investigating the insurrection, pointed to an email from Trump's Chief of Staff Mark Meadows that Meadows sent to an unnamed individual about the events of January 6th. In that email, according to a report by the committee, Meadows stated that, "the

National Guard would be present to 'protect pro Trump people' and that many more would be available on standby."

Meadows' comment makes another piece of Miller's May 2021 testimony stand out. He said that, in a phone call on January 5th, Trump suggested that ten-thousand Guard troops might be necessary the following day.

Again, that matters because Trump saw the Guard as a force that could be deployed to do "whatever was necessary to protect" those supporters he'd summoned to Washington.

If Miller took Trump's comments literally, he was in an impossible position. Trump didn't want the Guard deployed to battle the rioters. He wanted the Guard to keep them safe, perhaps, even, to support them.

Once the DC National Guard was deployed to the Capitol, Trump could have changed their mission from protecting the Capitol to what he'd previously told Miller (and, apparently, Meadows), he wanted them to do.

Miller hinted in his testimony that he worried about rumblings that the military would be used to help effect an insurrection. That would have allowed Trump to invoke the Insurrection Act. While he didn't dwell on the issue, and no congressional questioner pressed him on it, this might have been Miller's entire rationale for inaction.

Later, the world would learn how close Trump actually came to deploying the military to help him stay in power. The ideas tossed around went beyond invoking the Insurrection Act. Advisers had recommended additional roles for the military, specifically, the National Guard, as well as the secretary of defense. It's reasonable to assume that acting Secretary of Defense Christopher Miller was aware of these machinations, since they would have required him to implement them, including one proposal that came to light only after the Supreme Court rejected Trump's attempt to keep the January 6th

House Committee from viewing documents over which he asserted claims of executive privilege.

The scheme, laid out in a draft executive order, and never signed, was dated December 16, 2020, three weeks before the January 6th insurrection. The author of the draft hasn't been officially identified as of this writing, but available evidence suggests the involvement of Sidney Powell. She was reported to have met with Trump two days later, on December 18, 2020. During the meeting, *The New York Times* reported, Trump contemplated appointing Powell his "Special Counsel on Election Fraud."

Earlier that same week, retired Lieutenant General Michael Flynn, Trump's first national security adviser, and a client of Powell's, had raised the possibility on the extreme rightwing channel, *Newsmax*, of Trump declaring Martial Law and employing the military to re-run the election. Trump reportedly liked the idea—no surprise there. Flynn, who attended the December 18th meeting, reportedly endorsed Powell's plan. All others present, including Mark Meadows and Rudy Giuliani, who attended by phone, shot down Flynn's and Powell's recommendations. Loudly.

With the revelation of the never-signed executive order, it's possible to piece together how a plan could be so outrageous that not only would neither Giuliani nor Meadows endorse it, it triggered a shouting match.

The draft executive order, titled "PRESIDENTIAL FINDINGS TO PRESERVE COLLECT AND ANALYZE NATIONAL SECURITY INFORMATION REGARDING THE 2020 GENERAL ELECTION," claimed that voting machines used in the election were "intentionally and purposefully designed with inherent errors to create systemic fraud and influence election results," and that "there is probable cause to find a massive cyber-attack by foreign interests on our crucial national infrastructure surrounding our election."

AFTERMATH

Claims about foreign powers rigging the election via voting machines were standard Giuliani and Powell rhetoric. But the proposed remedy in the draft executive order was, indeed, novel.

It called for the Secretary of Defense (i.e., Christopher Miller), to deploy the National Guard to immediately seize all machines, equipment, electronically stored information, and records used in the 2020 election. The Department of Defense would analyze the materials and equipment and report its findings to the Office of the Director of National Intelligence within sixty days—long after Biden's January 20th inauguration date.

The draft order included a provision to appoint a "Special Counsel to oversee this operation and institute all criminal and civil proceedings as appropriate based on the evidence collected and provided all resources necessary to carry out her duties consistent with federal laws and the Constitution."

Note that the special counsel to be appointed under this draft order would have been carrying out "her" duties, suggesting that the draft either originated with Powell or contemplated Powell in that role. It all ties together with, and adds context to, what had been previously reported about the Trump-Powell meeting.

(In a different never-signed executive order draft, the Department of Homeland Security would have been authorized to seize the voting machines. Using this agency was, reportedly, Giuliani's preference.)

If reporters were able to ferret out as much as they did within a day of Trump's meeting with Powell, Giuliani, Meadows, and others, Miller, who would have been ordered to implement it had other advisers not shouted "Hell, no," almost certainly was briefed. Miller might have learned of other risks and plots, too, that nobody bothered to write down.

And yet, when he was asked during his congressional testimony, "Do you believe President Trump fulfilled his oath to faithfully execute

139

his duties as President and to preserve, protect, and defend the Constitution?" Miller answered, "Yes."

Was that answer simply political ass-covering?

And could Miller, via foot-dragging, and despite later ass-covering statements, have actually been attempting to save the country from a full-blown coup?

As yet, there's not enough evidence to be certain how to characterize his (in)actions.

In July 2021, after Senate Republicans blocked the creation of a bipartisan 9/11-style commission to investigate January 6th, Speaker Pelosi set up a House Select committee to do so. The committee was to have eight members appointed by Pelosi and five appointed by House Minority Leader Kevin McCarthy. Among Pelosi's choices for the committee were seven Democrats—three from California including Adam Schiff, Zoe Lofgren, and Pete Aguilar—along with Jamie Raskin of Maryland, Stephanie Murphy of Florida, and Elaine Luria of Virginia. Bennie Thompson of Mississippi acted as chair. She also chose one Republican, Liz Cheney of Wyoming. Republicans in the House had previously stripped Cheney of her position as minority conference chair, a leadership position, for her outspoken condemnation of Trump, and her vote to impeach him.

Among McCarthy's five picks for the select committee was Jim Jordan (R-OH), an ally of Trump's who, at minimum, was a material witness to attempts to keep Trump in power despite his loss, and who some suspected played a more active role. Pelosi vetoed him as well as one other McCarthy appointee, Jim Banks (R-IN). In retaliation, Minority Leader McCarthy refused to allow any Republicans to serve.

Still, Adam Kinzinger of Illinois agreed to be the second Republican select committee member. Kinzinger also had voted to impeach Trump for inciting the insurrection. Months later, the Republican National

Committee (RNC) would censure both Republicans for serving on the House Select Committee, claiming that "Representatives Cheney and Kinzinger are participating in a Democrat-led persecution of ordinary citizens engaged in legitimate political discourse, and they are both utilizing their past professed political affiliation to mask Democrat abuse of prosecutorial power for partisan purposes."

But when the committee began its public work with a hearing on July 27, 2021, it became apparent that this was a serious investigation into a devastating event.

Committee Chairman Bennie Thompson set the tone by displaying a montage of video from January 6th, much of it either filmed and posted by insurrectionists, or from officers' body-worn cameras. The video showed members of the January 6th mob rampaging through the building, brutally attacking the cops guarding the lower west terrace tunnel, chanting a call to murder Mike Pence, and threatening to hunt down lawmakers "one-by-one."

As vice-chair of the committee, Congresswoman Liz Cheney's opening statement admonished members of her own party who'd sought to minimize what happened on January 6th: "No member of Congress should now attempt to defend the indefensible, obstruct this investigation or whitewash what happened that day. We must act with honor and duty and in the interest of our nation."

Moments later, four police officers who had responded to the insurrection began their dramatic first-person testimony.

Sergeant Aquilino Gonell of the Capitol Police spoke first.

He recounted his history as an immigrant from the Dominican Republic who was thrilled to have emigrated to the US, the land of opportunity, and who had fulfilled dreams that family members could only imagine: becoming a US citizen, becoming the first in his family to graduate college, and earning promotions in the army and in the Capitol Police to the rank of sergeant.

When it came time to speak of January 6th, he choked up.

It was simply inconceivable to him that fellow citizens of his adopted country could attack their own government, their own law enforcement, calling him and other cops traitors to the Constitution that they were, at that very moment, risking their lives to defend.

And he spoke about how when the siege was finally over, and he was able to return home the next morning after 4:00 am, longing for the comfort of his wife's caress, he was unable to hug her because his uniform was saturated with chemicals that could harm her—bear spray, tear gas, pepper spray. The residue burned his skin even after he showered, making it impossible to sleep. But he got up again and headed back to the Capitol by 8:00 am, because he knew he was needed.

After working fifteen days straight, he was forced to attend to the injuries he suffered fighting back the insurrectionists and to take a medical leave until his wounds healed, which they hadn't yet as of the hearing.

Beyond the physical trauma, the wounds to his spirit had not mended. He asked the committee for justice, accountability.

MPD Officer Michael Fanone was the next to testify. He spoke of the brutal attack by the mob and his realization of how close he had come to being torn apart and killed. But there was a sense, in his monologue, that as horrendous as that experience was, he was able to process it more easily than the sense of betrayal he felt when lawmakers and others treated what cops had suffered on January 6th dismissively for the sake of politics.

"Nothing, truly nothing, has prepared me to address those elected members of our government who continue to deny the events of that day, and in doing so betray their oath of office, those very members whose lives, offices, staff members, I was fighting so desperately to defend."

Fanone was followed by MPD Officer Daniel Hodges, who recounted being attacked multiple times before he was nearly crushed to death when trapped in the doorway of the lower west terrace tunnel. Last to testify was Capitol Police Officer Harry Dunn, who had guarded the steps that led down to the lower west terrace tunnel to ensure that rioters already in the building couldn't attack the officers defending the tunnel from the other side. Dunn spoke of being sprayed with chemicals and attacked while enduring a stunning stream of racial slurs and abuse from the mob.

Once the Capitol was finally cleared, he said, he sat on a bench in the Rotunda, overcome by the horrors he'd seen and experienced that day, and cried out, "Is this America?"

Then he sobbed.

More than eight-hundred-fifty Metropolitan Police answered the call to assist the Capitol Police. More than one-hundred-forty officers from both forces were physically injured, some grievously. The Department of Justice estimates that there were approximately one-thousand assaults on officers by members of the January 6th mob.

While battling insurgents in fierce hand-to-hand combat, both of Aquilino Gonell's hands were damaged, as well as his left shoulder, his left calf, and his right foot. As of the Select Committee hearing, he had undergone bone fusion surgery on the foot but still needed surgery to repair his shoulder.

After Michael Fanone's partner rushed him to the emergency room following his ordeal, Fanone was diagnosed with a heart attack, a concussion, and a traumatic brain injury.

Daniel Hodges' wounds included a concussion and multiple contusions.

Harry Dunn suffered emotional trauma that required extensive counseling.

The psychological damage inflicted on officers who were forced to battle their fellow citizens at the Capitol might linger the longest and for some, hurt the most, even if it's the least visible. Two officers who defended the Capitol committed suicide shortly afterwards. Numerous officers, traumatized by the events of January 6th, have left the force. It's impossible to know how many who remain on the job still suffer from trauma's after-effects.

The committee has done its work since the officers' testimony away from the cameras. By April 2022, its investigators had interviewed approximately eight hundred witnesses, including the former president's daughter, Ivanka Trump, who was in the White House during the insurrection and was reported to have tried to get Trump to call it off, and her husband, Jared Kushner.

Committee investigators have also reviewed countless documents, including more than two-thousand turned over by former Trump chief of staff Mark Meadows. Meadows stopped cooperating with the committee after providing the documents, but what he offered prior to withdrawing cooperation was significant. Of those made public, the most explosive were texts to and from Ginni Thomas, the Republican activist wife of Supreme Court Justice Clarence Thomas, in which she repeated conspiracy theories as if they were fact, including that "Biden and the Left is [sic] attempting the greatest Heist of our History."

In a text she sent to Meadows two days after the election, on November 5, 2020, she reportedly was quoting a rightwing website that claimed the Biden family and "ballot fraud co-conspirators (elected officials, bureaucrats, social media censorship mongers, fake stream media reporters, etc) are being arrested & detained for ballot fraud right now & over coming days, & will be living in barges off GITMO to face military tribunals for sedition." In yet another, sent after the insurrection, on January 10, 2021, she wrote that "Most of us are disgusted with the VP." That seems to indicate that the disgust had to with Pence's refusal, four days prior, to help Trump overturn the election.

The shock of learning that a Supreme Court justice's wife was eager to support a coup can overshadow a milder surprise: the Big Lie wasn't just swallowed by a majority of Republican voters. A Supreme Court justice's wife actually believed it, too (which makes one wonder about other prominent conservatives, including the justice, himself).

Like Meadows, a number of other top Trump allies have refused to cooperate with the January 6th Select Committee, or have invoked the fifth amendment against self-incrimination during depositions. While these include some of the highest profile members of Trump's circle, enough individuals have spoken openly with committee investigators to paint a relatively comprehensive picture of the plots and players involved in the attempt to overturn the election and overthrow the elected government.

And what became of those insurrectionists who breached the Capitol building? About eight-hundred had been charged by April 2022.

Most of the non-violent invaders who pleaded guilty plea-bargained down to minor offenses and received little and often no prison time.

QAnon devotee Doug Jensen, who led one of the first groups of rioters into the Senate side of the building and came close to encountering Vice President Pence, was indicted for several offenses, including obstruction of an official proceeding. He had been granted bail but it was revoked when he was discovered to have violated the terms of his release by viewing conspiracy websites while in his garage.

Jacob Chansley, the QAnon shaman, pleaded guilty to a single felony, obstructing an official proceeding, and was sentenced to forty-one months in prison. He has reportedly disavowed QAnon and henceforth wants to be known as simply a shaman.

Lonnie Leroy Coffman, who came to the Capitol on January 6th in a truck loaded with Molotov cocktails, unregistered guns, hundreds of rounds of ammunition, a stun gun, machetes, and a crossbow, pleaded guilty and was sentenced to forty-six months in prison.

Jessica Watkins, who believed her militia unit was being legally activated by Trump as part of his plan to invoke the Insurrection Act, was indicted, along with Oath Keepers' leader Stewart Rhodes and nine other members of the militia, for seditious conspiracy, among other crimes. On the seditious conspiracy count, alone, she and other Oath Keepers face potential sentences of up to twenty years if convicted.

Five Proud Boys were also charged with seditious conspiracy, including Dominic Pezzola, the first to break into the Capitol building by smashing a window with a police riot shield, Joseph Biggs, and Proud Boys leader Enrique Tarrio, who was arrested the day before the insurrection on other charges, which prevented him from joining Proud Boys who breached the Capitol on January 6th.

Ryan Nichols, dog rescuer turned new-1776 provocateur, was charged with obstruction of an official proceeding, among other offenses.

Danny Rodriguez who confessed to assaulting Officer Michael Fanone with a taser faces conspiracy and assault charges.

Thomas Sibick, accused of stealing Officer Fanone's badge and radio while others brutally assaulted the officer, asked a federal judge to allow him to use dating apps while on house arrest at his parents' home, awaiting trial.

With no charges pending and none, apparently, forthcoming, Donald J. Trump has continued, into 2022, to hold rallies around the country where he rants about how the election was stolen from him.

8

The Once and Future Coup

"*If Dr. Eastman and President Trump's plan had worked, it would have permanently ended the peaceful transition of power, undermining American democracy and the Constitution. If the country does not commit to investigating and pursuing accountability for those responsible, the Court fears January 6 will repeat itself.*"

— US District Court Judge David O. Carter, ruling that John Eastman must turn over documents to the House Committee investigating the January 6th attack

On September 23, 2020, about six weeks before election day, Barton Gellman's article, "The Election That Could Break America," was published online in *The Atlantic*. It included an accurate depiction of one facet of the Trump coup plan that Trump and his allies would later attempt to put in motion, exactly as predicted.

It went like this: if the vote didn't go Trump's way in states with majority Republican state legislatures, and Biden was declared the winner, the Trump campaign wanted those legislatures to claim that rampant fraud had tainted the election. They then wanted the Republican state legislators to say that since the vote couldn't be trusted, it was their duty to ignore it and substitute their own hand-chosen electors—who, of course, would cast the states' electoral ballots for Trump.

The publication date of Gellman's article is evidence that a Reichstag fire, to be lit by the man who would claim to be its victim, was being kindled long before the election.

But this vital intel didn't circulate very widely. As far as most of the public knew, the attempt to overturn the election began after election day, and was a court gambit: Trump's lawyers tried and failed to get courts to toss out the entire popular votes of several states on the most minor technicalities. The claims made in court cases were often reported by major media as ludicrous. But the ploy was always about getting state legislators to substitute their votes for everyone else in their respective state's vote when choosing electors. The courts were just one means of arriving at that destination.

For several days before the January 6th rally, Rudy Giuliani huddled at the Willard Hotel in a so-called war room with a number of other lawyers and Trump operatives including Roger Stone and Steve Bannon.

The goal, as Bannon put it, was "to kill the Biden presidency in the crib."

How did they imagine they could do that, so close to Biden's inauguration?

It goes back to what Barton Gellman's sources were telling him pre-election, and what the Department of Justice attorney, Jeffrey Clark, proposed to Trump in December 2020, when Clark tried to get acting Attorney General Rosen fired and have himself installed in his place: a radical reading of something called the Independent State Legislature Doctrine.

The Constitution lays out ground rules for presidential elections. Article II, Section 1 says that "Each state shall appoint, in such Manner as the Legislature thereof may direct, a Number of Electors" who ultimately cast votes for the president on behalf of their states. Collectively, these electors are what we call the electoral college.

State legislatures were given the absolute power by this section of the Constitution to decide how their electors were appointed. The legislatures of all fifty states long ago wrote laws that ceded that power to ordinary voters like you and me: electors would be chosen by popular vote. With that settled, most states also wrote rights and protections for voters into their constitutions.

But according to some of those who espouse the Independent State Legislature Doctrine, the rights of individual voters like you and me to cast votes and have those votes counted isn't all that settled. Under the doctrine, state legislatures could theoretically take back the power from voters. But there are different views of how far this right of state legislatures under Article II, Section 1 goes.

Most experts insist that there are limits: state legislatures would only be able to claw back voting rights from the people if a state's constitution doesn't specifically grant individual voters that right. In other words, the legislature can write a law to change election procedure, but if a new law was unconstitutional, per the state's constitution, it would be found invalid and have no effect.

Other experts claimed that because the federal Constitution under Article II, Section 1 gave the power to select the way electors are chosen to state legislatures, no one and nothing could constrain that right if the legislature decided to take it back and leave voters out of the equation. Not a governor's veto. Not the state's constitution. Not the courts.

But even those who claimed that state legislatures had the sole, absolute authority to decide how electors were chosen balked at the notion that state legislatures could simply cancel the results of an election they didn't like *after* voters had made their choice.

Such a reading was about as radical and unprecedented as the claim that the vice president could unilaterally overturn the election during certification.

Yet, that's exactly the position that some Trump loyalist lawyers took: that legislatures could throw out the popular vote, post-election, on whatever premise they chose.

And Trump and his allies were willing to test this interpretation because, why not? If they were later shot down by the Supreme Court, what did they have to lose in the meantime? Trump would be president until and unless the Supreme Court ruled otherwise.

Trump's tweet at 2:24 pm on January 6th, might have had a dual purpose: to remind state legislators that he was counting on them, and to remind supporters, including those invading the Capitol at that moment, that the vice president wasn't cooperating with his schemes:

"Mike Pence didn't have the courage to do what should have been done to protect our Country and our Constitution, giving States a chance to certify a corrected set of facts, not the fraudulent or inaccurate ones which they were asked to previously certify. USA demands the truth!"

"The states"—or at least the officials in charge of certifying the states' election results, whether Democrats or Republicans—wanted to do no such thing. Overturning the will of the majority of voters would mean collaborating in a coup.

But in seven states—Arizona, Georgia, Michigan, Nevada, New Mexico, Pennsylvania, and Wisconsin—Trump supporters had already clumsily been putting the plan into place that Barton Gellman's sources for his *The Atlantic* article had alerted him to. They assembled what they claimed were rival slates of electors. These unofficial "electors" met, "cast" their votes for Trump, and attempted to transmit those votes to Washington.

What Trump and his allies still needed were enough state legislators in enough states to back these rogue electors.

On January 2nd, four days before the Save America rally, Trump, Giuliani, and John Eastman, a former clerk to Justice Clarence Thomas, who figured heavily in the attempts to overturn the election, were among those on a conference call with as many as three-hundred Republican state legislators.

Trump gave a fourteen-minute version of his "rigged election" spiel, with a demand to hand over the electoral votes of the states he'd lost so he could claim an eleventh hour victory. "You're the ones," Trump told the legislators on the call, "that are going to make the decision [to switch Biden electoral votes to Trump]."

What if enough had succumbed to Trump's demands?

More to the point, why should we assume that just because no state went along with canceling the popular vote in January 2021, none will in the future?

As noted earlier, the attempt to keep Trump in power was multi-faceted and included the outrageous claim that the vice president could unilaterally decide not to count all Biden ballots.

This parallel ploy was conjured up by John Eastman, who was, at the time, a law professor at Chapman University's School of Law (within a week of the rally, he "retired" under pressure).

Like the radical reading of the Independent State Legislature Doctrine, it required revoking state certifications of election results in several states that Trump lost.

But where the Independent State Legislature plan required the collusion of state lawmakers, Eastman's more streamlined version circumvented the need to persuade any new accomplices at the state level.

Under Eastman's theory, Vice President Mike Pence, whose ceremonial role was limited to ascertaining and acknowledging the states' certifications, would take the position that he had sole authority to decide which states' electoral votes counted.

It should be obvious to anyone that this has never been the interpretation of US presidential election law. Otherwise, Al Gore could have declared himself president in 2000 and avoided all the bother of court cases.

Eastman dismissed the Electoral College Act, a nineteenth century law which detailed the means of counting electoral college ballots, as unconstitutional. He claimed that Pence could ignore the law.

That left the twelfth amendment to the Constitution, which lays out, in far less detail than the Electoral College Act, the manner in which presidents and vice presidents are to be certified by Congress (Note that the vice president of the United States also has the title, president of the Senate). It reads, in part:

"The President of the Senate shall, in the presence of the Senate and House of Representatives, open all the certificates and **the votes shall then be counted**." [emphasis added]

The loophole Eastman apparently believed he found arose from the passive voice in the last phrase of the above sentence: "the votes shall then be counted." The amendment doesn't say who does the counting. Congress has always been involved in the count. In Eastman's reading, the way the amendment was written meant the vice president, as "President of the Senate," could simply declare that he had sole authority to decide which votes he would accept—and there would be nothing in the constitutional language to refute him.

Given this novel interpretation, Pence was supposed to claim that he could not determine who won the electoral votes of the seven states where bogus electors had essentially appointed themselves. Nevermind that the seven states, like all the others, had already certified their true electors.

Pence would set aside those states' votes entirely, accepting only the electoral votes of states with no rival (sham) slates of electors.

The votes of those seven states wouldn't count at all.

The result, had Pence gone along with the scheme, after removing the seven states from the tally, would be 232 electoral votes for Trump versus 222 for Biden, making Trump the winner of the majority.

Eastman knew that Democrats would revolt at such a flagrant coup attempt. But he anticipated that, when they did, the chaos created by a vice president's attempt to usurp authority would create such a crisis that the House of Representatives would be forced to determine who should be president.

At the time, Democrats held a majority in the House. But that wouldn't have given them the majority in the vote that determined who won the presidency because of a quirk in the way another section of the twelfth amendment to the Constitution was written:

"...the person having the greatest number of votes for President, shall be the President... But in choosing the President, the votes shall be taken by states, **the representation from each state having one vote.***"* [emphasis added]

Those last eight words in the last sentence meant that no matter how many Congressional representatives a state might have, for the purpose of deciding a disputed presidential election, each state delegation got only a single vote. So California, with its fifty-three-person delegation, representing nearly forty million people, got just one vote. Wyoming, with its one-person delegation, representing fewer than six hundred-thousand people, also got one vote.

In the longer of the two memos he wrote about this scheme, Eastman pointed out that Republicans held the majority in twenty-six of the fifty states' delegations, and anticipated that all twenty-six of those Republican-majority states would cast their votes for Trump, cementing his hold on the presidency for another four years.

There are, however, many reasons why this probably wouldn't have worked for the 2020 election, even if Pence had agreed to the plan.

It's true that Republicans controlled twenty-six of the fifty state House Congressional delegations. Democrats controlled just twenty-two, and two delegations, Michigan and Pennsylvania, included an even number of Republicans and Democrats. But that doesn't mean that all Republican members would have been willing to sign on to Trump's coup, any more than Pence was.

It's impossible to know for certain how individual congressional members would have voted, if it came to that. We do, however, have clues. Although the majority of Republican congressional representatives voted to object to certifying Biden as president, *not all of them* did. It's unlikely that someone who resisted the pressure to object to certification would succumb to the pressure to overthrow the duly elected president.

In each of the two states with half Democratic and half Republican members, at least one Republican chose not to object, resulting in the majority voting to certify Biden's win. In Wisconsin and Georgia, where Republicans outnumbered Democrats, the majority still voted to certify.

Wyoming's one-person congressional delegation in January 2021 consisted entirely of Liz Cheney.

Liz Cheney, too, voted to certify, posting the following in a tweet the morning of January 6th:

"Congress has no authority to overturn elections by objecting to electors. Doing so steals power from the states & violates the Constitution."

In all, the majority of members in twenty-seven state delegations voted to certify the electoral college vote. This is the opposite of how both Eastman and Clark anticipated the vote would go when they promoted their coup-via-Congress plans.

In a January 4, 2021 meeting with Pence's chief counsel, Greg Jacobs, described as "intense," Eastman acknowledged that Pence didn't have unilateral authority to toss out electoral votes after all, despite the

THE ONCE AND FUTURE COUP

claims in his memo. But that memo also outlined a fallback position. Pence should, he said, unilaterally adjourn the January 6th joint session of Congress, until each of the legislatures of the seven states with self-appointed electors had time to "investigate" which slate to certify.

Meanwhile, Trump would remain in the White House.

Eastman apparently expected enough state legislatures to switch to the rogue electors to give Trump another four years.

Pence didn't go along with that plan, either.

So, Eastman's multiple ploys failed, just as Clark's had.

Before anyone relaxes, this means only that these plots failed in that particular year.

As for subsequent elections, might different people be weighing their options, and elaborating on and refining Eastman's and Clark's schemes?

What could happen then is anyone's guess.

A key question is how the January 6th Save America rally and storming of the Capitol fit into the plan for Trump to hold onto the presidency after losing the election, assuming it did. Would it have been enough just to stop Congress from certifying the vote that day? Not really. Congress could resume another day. The election results would not change.

In order for Trump to hold onto power, the popular vote in a number of states had to be discarded and the states' electoral college votes nullified.

We know that Trump and his allies saw the events of that day as their last, best chance to make that happen, because they said so. The question, after Pence refused to go along, is how?

Steve Bannon, who had been part of the Trump administration when Trump took office but was fired about eight months later, was part of the Willard Hotel war room assembly. Bannon had apparently returned to Trump's inner circle of advisers during the campaign and appears to have had an expanded role in the lead-up to January 6th. On his podcast, War Room, the day before, he suggested Trump supporters show up on January 6th with comments like this:

"So many people have said, 'Man, if I was in a revolution, I would be in Washington.' Well, this is your time in history."

And this:

"It's all converging, and now we're on the point of attack tomorrow."

That sounded more like an invitation to battle than a request to show up for speeches by your favorite politicians. But the question still is, how were all those Trump supporters descending on the Capitol supposed to help ensure that Trump retained power?

One theory is that Team Trump expected a battle between the rioters and a competing army of counter-protesters consisting of an amalgam of anti-racist, anti-fascist, and other anti-Trump groups. Trump supporters, especially members of the Proud Boys, have often clashed with left-leaning demonstrators. Oath Keepers, in their communications, expressly spoke of preparing to do battle on the streets of DC with such anti-Trump forces. Others, not affiliated with any organized group, including Danny Rodriguez, also expected to fight with adversaries from the left.

But the counter-protesters, for the most part, failed to show up on January 6th.

The mob that overran police and stormed the Capitol was quite clearly made up of Trump supporters and only Trump supporters, save for one lone man from Utah who claimed to be anti-fascist and a supporter of Black Lives Matter, but also said he was there as a journalist to chronicle events.

One way this theory might fit is this: Prior to January 6th there had been a good deal of chatter about Trump invoking the Insurrection Act, declaring martial law, and hanging onto power, at least temporarily, by suspending civil rights. A number of Trump's supporters, including his first National Security Adviser, Michael Flynn, promoted such a scenario. The Insurrection Act would allow the president to use the military to put down a rebellion. First, of course, he needed the rebellion. And Trump, intentionally or not, supplied his own, with his message to supporters to come to DC on the 6th to "stop the steal" and "be wild."

Trump's tweet, "Mike Pence didn't have the courage to do what should have been done to protect our Country and our Constitution... " was posted soon after the rioters breached the building. Trump knew they were in the Capitol at that moment, searching for his vice president. And Pence was not yet in his secure underground location, though his detail would move him within two minutes of the tweet.

How did Trump expect the mob he'd mustered to react to that statement?

The insurrectionists didn't seem to know quite what to do inside when they failed to find either Pence or any lawmakers. The police they assaulted, sometimes viciously, were impediments to their objectives. Punishing Pence *was* one of the objectives. If Pence had become a captive, or worse, had been assassinated, would that have given Trump the opening he needed?

About a month after the Capitol siege, Ryan Grim, writing in *The Intercept,* mused that turning a potentially murderous band of insurgents against his vice president would have served Trump's immediate goal, and might even have been part of his strategy. If insurrectionists killed or badly injured Pence, could the certification even have gone forward?

The vice president had a role laid out by the Constitution in certifying the ballots. No vice president—no certification.

Grim speculated that such an event would have given Trump the chance to declare a state of emergency, and thereby live "to fight another day."

His scenario, at first glance, seemed implausible. But in a public hearing of the January 6th House Select Committee, Congresswoman Liz Cheney claimed that Trump knew of the rioters' "Hang Mike Pence" chant, and responded that "Maybe our supporters have the right idea." Trump denied saying or even thinking such a thing.

With Pence's capture—or worse—Trump would have a rationale for invoking the Insurrection Act.

Or the plan might have been, as some have suggested, simply to get Pence out of the building and make it difficult or impossible for him to return, at least right away.

Only Trump knows what Trump was thinking, but Grim was right that he seemed desperate to delay certification, even if only briefly. We know this because at about seven o'clock on the evening of January 6th, while the Capitol was still locked down and lawmakers were sheltering in place, waiting for the all-clear to resume debate on certifying Arizona's electoral votes, Giuliani called Senator Mike Lee's phone. Like Trump had earlier that day, Giuliani mistakenly believed he was dialing Senator Tommy Tuberville's number. The call went to voice mail.

Senator Lee apparently forwarded Giuliani's voice mail to the newsletter, *The Dispatch*, which published the recording in its entirety, along with a transcript.

The Capitol had already been cleared of insurrectionists by the time of his call, but Giuliani was still begging Tuberville to help further delay the certification.

And now, Giuliani was asking Tuberville to object, not just to the seven states with bogus electors, but to add another three states to the objection list, and get a House rep to go along with the new objections, which would force two hours of debate on each one. Though, in his voice mail, Giuliani didn't identify the three new states he wanted added to the objection list, he did say he needed Tuberville to push the vote back as far as possible—ideally until the end of the day on January 7th. He claimed that some state legislators were very close to "pulling their vote": in other words, canceling the popular vote in their state(s).

Until this call, only seven states were publicly being targeted by Trump allies. Which were the other three states? And were Giuliani and Trump actually that close to succeeding at a self-coup via a radical reading of the Independent State Legislature Doctrine?

On the Senate floor that night, after the siege had ended and the chamber had reconvened to continue debating the certification of electoral ballots, Senator Lee rose to say that, over the last few weeks, he had reached out to state legislators, governors, and others with roles to play in the election in states that Trump and his allies contested. In none—"Not even one"—did he find that state officials wanted to alter the slate of electors already certified.

Who was right, Giuliani or Lee?

Trump's post-2020 election self-coup attempt failed.

But having exposed a number of weak points in the system, Trump and his allies have made a future coup more likely, and also more likely to succeed. And that is true, whether Trump runs again or it's someone else.

The next coup attempt, if based upon the Independent State Legislature Doctrine, and set in motion well in advance of an election, might bypass courts altogether. Or a court case might be brought simply to get sympathetic judges to affirm the radical notion that only state legislatures have any authority to decide anything, at any time, about who gets to allocate electoral votes. If a majority of justices on the highest court in the country should find that a persuasive argument, state constitutional provisions that protect the rights of citizens to vote might be moot.

Though the Trump coup attempt looked, at times, like a bumbling clown show, Giuliani, Clark, Eastman, and other lawyers involved deserve some kind of credit for uncovering so many ways to potentially overthrow the United States government. The problem with their maneuvers wasn't necessarily that they were dead on arrival, as some legal experts claim. The coup failed mostly because a few principled Republicans believed in our current system, and were more committed to that system than to Trump.

That might not always be the case.

Election laws in a number of states have since been changed in ways that will make it more difficult to vote, and will also give partisans more power to undermine the vote. Among proposed new state laws are ones that diminish the authority of state and local election officials, and increase the state legislature's power to overturn an election after it's been held.

A handful of principled people in the right positions saved the system in 2020. Substitute a handful of unprincipled people in the right positions, and voting might no longer matter.

Trumpism has changed the country and especially, the Republican party, in a stunningly brief period of time. Consider a *Politico* article from June 2019 that asked: "What If Trump Won't Accept 2020 Defeat?" The article went on to quote various people who scoffed at the question, for example, Senator Roy Blunt (R-MO), who responded, "Of all the silly things that are being said, that may be the silliest." Ohio Republican Congressman Steve Chabot also weighed in, saying, "There's no chance of anything like that possibly happening. That's just hysteria. No way would that ever happen."

A little more than eighteen months later, that same Congressman Chabot joined the effort to overturn the election results in Pennsylvania.

Emboldened by Trump's disregard for all norms, laws, and traditions—or cowed by Trump's ability to destroy careers and lives with a single comment—the risk-reward ratio for anyone with a role in election-related decisions has changed from what it once was.

That might still be true if Trump is no longer in the picture, because others, seeing a winning formula, likely will emulate him.

And it's not just the potential future actions of anti-democratic politicians that inject greater uncertainty into the system.

In late November 2020, the home of Georgia Secretary of State Brad Raffensperger's widowed daughter-in-law was broken into. That same night, people who identified themselves to the police as Oath Keepers were found scoping out the elder Raffenspergers' home. These incidents were seen as payback after Raffensperger refused to "find" extra ballots that didn't exist so that Georgia's electoral votes could be switched from Biden to Trump. The Raffenspergers went into hiding for a brief period of time. But the threats didn't stop. More than six months after the 2020 election, Raffensperger's wife received a text saying: "You and your family will be killed very slowly." As of September 2021, Trump was still attacking Raffensperger by name at rallies.

There were also bomb threats against Georgia's polling places. An email about bombing these locales read, in part: "No one at these places will be spared unless and until Trump is guaranteed to be POTUS again."

Local officials, even lowly poll workers, have been targeted. Two black women were among election workers counting Fulton County, Georgia's mail-in ballots for the 2020 election. Giuliani, other Trump allies, and even Trump, himself, falsely claimed the women were counting "suitcases" of illegal ballots that had been hidden from election monitors. In reality, the women, following protocol, had retrieved sealed packages of ordinary mail-in ballots that had been stored properly while ballot counting was paused. All their actions, from sealing to retrieving the ballots, were documented on video and clearly shown to be legal and proper. But the women were threatened so often after the false accusations, with death threats tinged with racial slurs, they were forced into hiding.

The secretaries of state in both Michigan and Arizona also reported ongoing threats related to the 2020 election. Trump lost both states but insisted that he'd won them.

After so many election workers and officials suffered menace and abuse from Trump's supporters after his relentless verbal attacks, how will future officials manage the peril?

While we don't usually think of governors as election officials, the governor must sign a certificate of ascertainment before the state's electoral votes can be sent to Washington, DC. Trump verbally attacked Georgia's Republican governor, Brian Kemp, who refused to pretend to believe Trump's claims of rigging. Might a different governor have calculated that it would be easier to simply refuse to sign the certificate? Could anyone force the governor to do so, if the governor refused?

Election lawyer Marc Elias, in his newsletter, *Democracy Docket*, wrote that, without the certificate of ascertainment, signed by the governor, the electoral votes of Georgia probably would not have been counted at all. Elias also pointed out that had Kemp refused to sign the certificates of election for Raphael Warnock and Jon Ossoff, the two new Democratic senators from Georgia who won in 2020, it's unlikely that either would have been seated in the Senate.

Of course, Kemp and all other governors in 2020 followed the law and the will of the voters of their respective states. But what might future governors do under similar duress?

When we look at how many other Republican politicians embraced—or at least, failed to vociferously reject—a Big Lie they must have realized was built on a foundation of vanity and bile, we can see how lucky we were in 2020, insurrection notwithstanding.

House Minority Leader Kevin McCarthy had this to say a week after the siege of the Capitol: "The president bears responsibility for Wednesday's attack on Congress by mob rioters." In addition to calling for Trump to be censured for his role in inciting the January 6th mob, McCarthy initially called for an independent investigation into the insurrection. Under pressure from Trump, he reversed himself on all of that.

Senator Lindsey Graham (R-SC) performed perhaps the most enduring and infamous backflip in his relationship with the real estate hustler turned politician. Here was Graham in December 2015:

"You know how you make America great again? Tell Donald Trump to go to hell. He's a race-baiting, xenophobic, religious bigot. He doesn't represent my party. He doesn't represent the values that the men and women who wear the uniform are fighting for."

But after Trump won in 2016, Graham ingratiated himself with the new president, became an adviser, became a golfing buddy, became a vocal supporter of Trump's re-election, and even suggested in an interview with Fox TV's Sean Hannity that some of the Trumpist vote rigging claims might be valid. He also seemed to have forgotten his original judgment when he responded to a question about whether Trump was racist for telling four congresswomen of color, in 2019, to go back where they came from. "If you think he's a racist, that's up to you—I don't."

Some of those lawmakers who objected to certifying Biden's win might have been getting their "news" from the same dubious sources as the insurrectionists, and might have had genuine concerns about the integrity of the election. But, even giving a handful the benefit of the doubt, a far greater number were probably, like Lindsey Graham, going along to get along. A few such people are all it would take to end the current system of elections in the United States of America.

And none of the above considers what would happen in the still un-likely—but no longer completely implausible—event that the military got involved.

In May 2021, one-hundred-twenty-four retired generals and admirals signed an unprecedented letter that gave full-throated support to Trump's Big Lie. Their letter also accused President Biden and Democrats in Congress of having taken "a hard left turn toward socialism and a Marxist form of tyrannical government." Because none of those who signed the letter was actively serving or recently retired, many current military leaders dismissed the concern that the group's members could sway others. But their claims could be seen as a rationale for a military coup. And that's something that can't be so easily dismissed.

Alarmed by such rumblings among retired military brass, a different trio of former generals co-wrote a December 2021 *Washington Post* op ed in which they pointed out related risks, including: "The potential for a total breakdown of the chain of command along partisan lines." Among their concerns: more than ten percent of the insurrectionists charged in the January 6th siege were military veterans.

They also found it disturbing that, more recently, Brigadier General Thomas Mancino, the commanding general of Oklahoma's National Guard, refused to enforce President Biden's Covid-19 vaccine mandate for all troops. Mancino claimed that the state's governor, not the president, was his commander-in-chief, and the governor's were the orders he would be following.

With the perils to future elections so plentiful, are ironclad safeguards possible? Numerous experts and lawmakers have put forth proposals to mitigate the risks, if not completely eliminate them.

One that has been around far longer than Trump would, for the first time in United States history, give voters the opportunity to directly choose their president. It's called the National Popular Vote Interstate Compact, and it would ensure that the winner of the popular vote would also win the electoral college vote. More, in a moment, about how it would work. But here's why it makes sense.

Under the current system, the loser of the popular vote can still win the presidency. It happened in 2000, when Al Gore won the popular vote by more than half a million but lost the electoral college vote to George W. Bush. It happened again in 2016, when Hillary Clinton beat Donald Trump by almost three million in the popular vote but lost the electoral college vote. And in 2020, although Biden won the electoral college vote, and won the popular vote by more than seven million, a shift of less than fifty thousand votes in Arizona, Georgia, and Wisconsin, would have canceled out a seven million vote advantage.

Is this a system we actually *want* to save? Can we call it a democracy?

We're stuck with the electoral college unless we eliminate it through a constitutional amendment. That's unlikely to happen. But the National Popular Vote Interstate Compact would provide a work-around. Once enough states sign on that control a total of two-hundred-seventy electoral college votes (the minimum number a candidate needs to win the presidency), all those states signing the compact agree to have their presidential electors cast their electoral votes for the winner of the national popular vote, no matter who won the popular vote in their respective states. The election would go to the choice of the majority across the nation.

Currently, fifteen states plus the District of Columbia, which together control a total of one-hundred-ninety-five electoral votes, have signed on. The compact won't go into effect until enough states to reach two-hundred-seventy sign on. At that point, assuming all goes as planned, the winner of the national popular vote would be assured of the presidency and even with the antiquated electoral college system still in place, the US would become a true democracy.

But even such a simple, elegant solution might be thwarted if there were a push to nullify the popular vote in any state in the compact by its legislature. Before 2020, that would have been unthinkable. Going forward, there are those who will view it as a useful tool to keep in the back pocket, should democracy get in the way of the preferences of the powerful.

There is no question that, as the House Articles of Impeachment against him stated, "President Trump...threatened the integrity of the democratic system, interfered with the peaceful transition of power, and imperiled a coequal branch of Government."

Simple agreement with these obvious facts would have led to Trump's conviction for high crimes and misdemeanors. The practical effect of his conviction would have been disqualification from "hold[ing] and enjoy[ing] any office of honor, trust, or profit under the United States."

Two-thirds of the Senate would have needed to have voted to convict in order to have prevented Trump from ever running for office again. Forty-three senators decided their personal ambitions eclipsed the need to protect the country from the return of a would-be dictator who tried to steal the office of the president for himself when he could not win it legally.

If there are no consequences for an attempted coup, why wouldn't he try it again? Why would the next would-be autocrat hesitate?

The only people who have been held to account—although, for the most part, quite minimally—were those who stormed the Capitol. They believed they were acting on the orders of their president. But their president, after entirely escaping punishment, or even much rebuke, went right back to promoting his Big Lie, and apparently, back to plotting to take back the presidency. By any means available.

Lawmakers who conspired with Trump to overthrow his successor still serve in Congress. In the next Congress, assuming Republicans regain the majority, these lawmakers will gain more power.

A great many experts warn that democracy will be soon coming to an end in the US unless those with the power to save it take action to do so. Those with the power to save it, however, don't appear to see how saving democracy might have greater value (to themselves, at least) than letting it die.

But democracy, operating on a constitutional foundation that protects individual rights and freedom, is almost certainly the best of all possible systems for the greatest number of us.

Democracy vests political power in all citizens.

Maybe the reason that a majority of senators, and others with the power to do so, have thus far refused to protect US democracy is because our version is so flawed. Throughout our history, including now, unfairness, even cheating, has been built into our system. Big "donors" contribute hundreds of millions of dollars to the campaigns of thousands of politicians. Politicians then return the favors, once in office, by voting for laws that further enrich those donors—or by failing to vote for laws that would cost those donors money. Because this is legal, it isn't called bribery. But it would be difficult to articulate a more fitting label.

That ocean of money keeps power in the hands of the few, whose interests differ from those of their presumed constituents. Bribery on a small scale might get a person arrested and imprisoned, but on the grander scale of political quid pro quo, it gets the person paying virtually anything the bought-and-sold politician is capable of delivering.

If legalized bribery decides which of our proposed laws get enacted (or fail to get enacted) can you call that democracy?

The idealized concept of democracy is a system in which no one gets to employ shortcuts, loopholes, technicalities, or oceans of cash to thwart the will of the majority. A democracy accepts majority rule, even when inconvenient or disappointing.

With a democracy already so corrupted, so unresponsive to the will of the majority, it might have been naïve to assume that all of us were as invested in it as imagined.

Maybe a society that venerates capitalism, that puts rapacious billionaires on pedestals, isn't cut out for a democracy that gives a say to the poorest among us.What could be less compatible with a find-the-loophole and win-at-all-costs ethos than a commitment to fairness and equal opportunity?

But even if all we have is the conceit of a democracy, the hint of it, do we want to let that vestige go? If we don't preserve what little we have, nurture it, and expand upon it, we're going to miss it when it's gone. Though our system has often failed to deliver, it hasn't been due to the democracy's flaws but due to the subversion of democracy's ideal.

Renouncing what's left of representative democracy in the United States of America, as lawmakers in DC are passively doing by their inaction, would eventually amount to losses for all but the smallest minority: the authoritarian at the top.

An old joke comes to mind about a guy who tells his girlfriend that if they marry, they can't have kids because insanity runs in his family. His brother is so crazy, he tells her, that he imagines himself a chicken. Alarmed, his girlfriend insists he get help for his brother. Can't do it, replies the fellow. "We need the eggs."

Abandoning democracy for what might be only an imaginary, or at best, fleeting advantage is true madness. If we continue on this path, our losses will be profound.

Research Notes

Sources: Foreshadowing

Epigraph quote: Select Committee To Investigate The January 6th Attack On The U.S. Capitol, U.S. House Of Representatives, Washington, D.C. Interview Of: Richard Peter Donoghue Friday, October 1, 2021

Bartiromo and Giuliani, Sunday Morning Futures 11-15-20

Complaint: In The Superior Court Of The State Of Delaware Us Dominion, Inc., Dominion Voting Systems, Inc., and Dominion Voting Systems, Corporation, Plaintiffs, v. Fox News Network, LLC Friday, October 1, 2021

FAQ Smartmatic defamation suit against Fox: https://www.smartmatic.com/us/media/article/faq-defamation-lawsuit-against-fox-corporation/

3/8/2022 Decision + Order On Motion, Smartmatic USA Corp., Smartmatic International Holding B.V., and SGO Corporation Limited, Plaintiffs, -v- Fox Corporation, Fox News Network LLC, Lou Dobbs, Maria Bartiromo, Jeanine Pirro, Rudolph Giuliani and Sidney Powell, Defendants

Major voting technology companies in 2016: https://www.accesswire.com/471912/Voting-Technology-Companies-in-the-US—Their-Histories-and-Present-Contributions

1984 was the last year a Republican presidential candidate won Los Angeles: https://en.wikipedia.org/wiki/1984_United_States_presidential_election_in_California

Fox News, most watched news channel: https://www.adweek.com/tvnewser/2022-state-of-the-union-ratings-fox-news-is-most-watched-abc-is-no-1-among-adults-25-54/502440/

Major voting technology companies in 2016: https://www.accesswire.com/471912/Voting-Technology-Companies-in-the-US—Their-Histories-and-Present-Contributions

Four Seasons Total Landscaping press conference: https://nymag.com/intelligencer/2020/12/four-seasons-total-landscaping-the-full-est-possible-story.html

Four Seasons Total Landscaping press conference: https://www.thedailybeast.com/the-end-of-the-line-for-trumpland-is-a-poorly-rated-sex-shop-in-north-philly

Four Seasons Total Landscaping press conference: https://www.washingtonpost.com/lifestyle/style/four-seasons-total-landscaping-guiliani-trump-election/2020/11/08/3cf80056-2134-11eb-b532-05c751cd5dc2_story.html

Associated Press calls Pennsylvania for Biden: https://apnews.com/article/ap-called-pennsylvania-joe-biden-why-f7dba7b31bd21ec2819a

7ac9d2b028d3

Giuliani dripping hair dye Press conference: https://www.vanityfair.c
om/news/2020/11/rudy-giuliani-hair-dye-press-conference

"Dominion, Smartmatic, Sequoia, and Venezuela" November 2020
Trump campaign memo debunks Dominion/Smartmatic fraud allegations.

Maddow on Trump wanting to help Putin: https://www.msnbc.com/t
ranscripts/rachel-maddow-show/2017-02-27-msna968341

Trump: "Maybe we'll have to give that a shot someday." https://www.r
euters.com/article/us-trump-china/trump-praises-chinese-president-
extending-tenure-for-life-idUSKCN1GG015

46 states close non-essential businesses to stop spread of Covid-19:
https://abcnews.go.com/Health/states-shut-essential-businesses-map
/story?id=69770806

Capitol police whistleblower letter, September 2021, pointed out that
Pittman had intel on violence's likelihood, but didn't share with Sund
or others in command.

2020 election results: https://en.wikipedia.org/wiki/2020_United_St
ates_presidential_election

Official and Unofficial Timeline of Defense Department Actions on
January 6: https://www.justsecurity.org/76117/the-official-and-unof
ficial-timeline-of-defense-department-actions-on-january-6/

"Knock the crap out of" anyone ready to throw a tomato, Trump will pay legal fees: https://www.thedailybeast.com/cheats/2016/02/01/trump-i-ll-pay-for-protester-beatings

Trump tweet May 2020: https://www.thetrumparchive.com/

States that vote exclusively by mail: https://en.wikipedia.org/wiki/Postal_voting_in_the_United_States

Trump speech, Oshkosh, Wisconsin, August 2020: https://www.rev.com/blog/transcripts/donald-trump-speech-transcript-wisconsin-august-17

Sidney Powell's four independent election lawsuits: https://en.wikipedia.org/wiki/Sidney_Powell

Rudy Giuliani license to practice law suspended: Supreme Court of the State of New York: In the Matter of Rudolph W. Giuliani (Admitted As Rudolph William Giuliani), an attorney and counselor-at law: Attorney Grievance Committee For The First Judicial Department, Petitioner, Rudolph W. Giuliani,(OCA Atty. Registration No. 1080498), Respondent.

Judge Sanctions Sidney Powell: https://www.npr.org/2021/08/25/1031127113/judge-sanctions-trump-allies-and-orders-legal-education-for-failed-election-laws

Giuliani and co-counsel in Pennsylvania court, "not a fraud case": https://www.latimes.com/politics/story/2020-11-17/trump-election-lawsuits-fizzle-as-giuliani-appears-in-court-for-him

Court case in Pennsylvania re voter being able or not being able to correct early ballot: https://www.factcheck.org/2020/11/ballot-curin g-in-pennsylvania/

Ad urging Trump to declare martial law and suspend the Constitution: https://wethepeopleconvention.org/articles/WTPC-Urges-Limited-Martial-Law

Trump pressures DoJ; Clark letter re fraud/replacing electors; threatens to replace Rosen with Clark: Select Committee To Investigate The January 6th Attack On The U.S. Capitol, U.S. House Of Representatives, Washington, D.C., Interview Of: Jeffrey A. Rosen, Wednesday, October 13, 2021 *and* Select Committee To Investigate The January 6th Attack On The U.S. Capitol, U.S. House Of Representatives, Washington, D.C., Interview Of: Richard Peter Donoghue, Friday, October 1, 2021

Trump/Meadows to DoJ: investigate Italy/CIA satellite theory: https://www.theguardian.com/us-news/2021/jun/06/donald-tr ump-mark-meadows-doj-italygate

Trump tweet "Big protest on January 6th": https://www.thetrumparc hive.com/

Trump rally speech "They're not taking this White House": https://w ww.rev.com/blog/transcripts/donald-trump-rally-speech-transcript-dalton-georgia-senate-runoff-election

Oath Keepers' preparations for January 6th: https://www.vice.com/en /article/epd8x4/oath-keepers-talked-about-protecting-the-capitolbef ore-they-stormed-it *and* Grand Jury indictment, Seditious Conspiracy and other charges, January 12, 2022 United States Of America V. Elmer

Stewart Rhodes, Kelly Meggs, Kenneth Harrelson, Jessica Watkins, Joshua James, Roberto Minuta, Joseph Hackett, David Moerschel, Brian Ulrich, Thomas Caldwell and Edward Vallejo, Defendants

Congresswoman Frederica Wilson: https://19thnews.org/2021/03/fr ederica-wilson-capitol-riot/ *and* https://thehill.com/homenews/hous e/534468-democrats-point-fingers-on-whether-capitol-rioters-had-i nside-help *and* https://www.newsweek.com/after-she-challenged-t rumps-treatment-soldiers-family-rep-frederica-wilson-688374 *and* https://thehill.com/homenews/house/534295-lawmakers-warned-p olice-of-possible-attack-ahead-of-siege *and* https://www.nytimes.co m/2017/10/18/us/politics/congresswoman-wilson-trump-niger-call-widow.html

Congresswoman Maxine Waters: https://thehill.com/homenews/hou se/534468-democrats-point-fingers-on-whether-capitol-rioters-had-inside-help *and* http://seattlemedium.com/congresswoman-maxine-waters-warnings-to-u-s-capitol-police-chief-were-ignored/

Police Chief Sund February 2, 2021 letter to Nancy Pelosi on intelligence failures.

Capitol police whistleblower letter, September 28, 2021 to congressional leaders: Pittman had intel on violence's likelihood, but didn't share with Sund or others in command.

DHS knew there wouldn't be sufficient law enforcement, but those monitoring social media never issued reports/threat alerts: March 4, 2022, Homeland Security Inspector General's report.

DHS was focused on tying antifa to terrorism and Black Lives Matter protest: https://www.opb.org/article/2021/10/01/senior-homeland-security-leaders-pushed-unfounded-antifa-conspiracy-at-2020-portland-protests-report-states/

Whistleblower complaint, Brian Murphy, DHS, Principal Deputy Under Secretary Department Of Homeland Security Office Of Intelligence & Analysis, stating he was retaliated against for refusing to alter reports to mirror Trump's claims that antifa and BLM were the true domestic terror threat.

Pages H143-H147 From the Congressional Record Online, including FBI warnings about potential for violence on January 6th: https://www.congress.gov/117/crec/2021/01/12/modified/CREC-2021-01-12-pt1-PgH143.htm

"Operation Occupy the Capitols" Republican party poster: https://www.mediamatters.org/january-6-insurrection/several-gop-organizations-posted-flyer-facebook-calling-operation-occupy

Letter from Vinson & Elkins law firm to Congresswoman Maloney, House Oversight Committee, March 25, 2021, stating that Parler had forwarded posts with violent content to the FBI, regarding January 6th as early as December 22, 2020

Former US diplomat suggests Esper firing is foundation for Trump coup: https://www.baltimoresun.com/opinion/readers-respond/bs-ed-rr-trump-esper-coup-letter-20201112-i44zv3exajbdplxefneyo66vqm-story.html

Miller rescinded Walker's authority to respond: https://www.washingtonpost.com/national-security/dc-guard-capitol-riots-william-walker

-pentagon/2021/01/26/98879f44-5f69-11eb-ac8f-4ae05557196e_sto
ry.html *and* https://thehill.com/policy/defense/535888-dc-national-g
uard-commander-says-pentagon-restricted-his-authority-before-riot
and page 28, The Harder Right: An Analysis of a Recent DoD Inspector
General Investigation and Other Matters by Colonel Earl G. Matthews,
U.S. Army December 1, 2021

Congressional reps spot MAGA groups in Capitol, including restricted
areas, on January 5, 2020: https://19thnews.org/2021/03/norma-torr
es-capitol-riot/ *and* https://19thnews.org/2021/03/mikie-sherrill-ca
pitol-riot/

Sources: Gathering

Epigraph quote: Mark Meadows' texts with Mike Lee and Chip Roy:
https://www.cnn.com/2022/04/15/politics/read-mark-meadows-tex
ts-mike-lee-chip-roy/index.html

Alex Jones and InfoWars background: https://en.wikipedia.org/wiki/
InfoWars

Jan 5, 2021 Alex Jones rally in Freedom Plaza: https://www.nytimes.c
om/2021/01/05/us/politics/dc-protests.html

Owen Shroyer called for Barack Obama to be lynched: https://www.n
ewsweek.com/infowars-host-owen-shroyer-calls-barack-obama-lyn
ched-find-tallest-tree-rope-1444987

Shroyer claimed Michelle Obama was a trans woman named Michael,
trying to sexualize children for demonic purposes: https://www.right

wingwatch.org/post/owen-shroyer-thinks-michelle-obama-is-a-tran
sgender-woman-seeking-to-implement-a-demonic-culture/

Shroyer promoted Pizzagate: https://www.salon.com/2019/12/09/in
fowars-host-who-called-for-obama-to-be-lynched-interrupts-impea
chment-hearing-trump-is-innocent/

Shroyer and Jones, Freedom Plaza, January 5, 2021: https://www.med
iamatters.org/media/3922181

AG Barr "flood the city" with 5,800 federal law enforcement for BLM
protests in June 2020: https://wamu.org/story/20/06/02/as-d-c-prot
ests-entered-fourth-day-trump-and-officials-didnt-miss-a-chance-to
-get-in-front-of-cameras/ and https://www.politifact.com/article/20
21/jan/08/black-lives-matter-protests-and-capitol-assault-co/

Trump: "We'll go into all the cities, any of the cities" https://www.was
hingtontimes.com/news/2020/jul/24/donald-trump-we-could-go-ci
ties-50k-75k-people-que/

Barr wanted to federalize DC Police (MPD) for BLM protests:
https://www.washingtonpost.com/local/public-safety/dc-police-
takeover-george-floyd/2020/06/02/856a9744-a4da-11ea-bb20-ebf0
921f3bbd_story.html

Letter, Mayor Bowser to DoJ: https://twitter.com/MayorBowser/stat
us/1346530358674792466

FBI report, videos, route pipe bomb suspect: https://www.fbi.gov/co
ntact-us/field-offices/washingtondc/news/press-releases/fbi-washin
gton-field-office-releases-video-and-additional-information-regardi

ng-the-pipe-bomb-investigation-090821

Capitol Police Chief Sund's plans for January 6th: February 2, 2021 Letter from Sund to Speaker Pelosi regarding Capitol security; *and* February 23, 2021 Testimony to Senate Rules Committee; *and* https://www.washingtonpost.com/politics/sund-riot-national-guard/2021/01/10/fc2ce7d4-5384-11eb-a817-e5e7f8a406d6_story.html and Capitol Police Whistleblower's letter of September 28, 2021 to Speaker Pelosi, Majority Leader Schumer, and House/Senate minority leaders.

Congressman Mo Brooks speech, Save America rally: https://www.youtube.com/watch?v=ZKHwV6sdrMk

Congresswoman Susan Wild: exclusive interview with Anita Bartholomew *and* https://www.penncapital-star.com/government-politics/stronger-together-pa-s-fab-four-women-lawmakers-make-their-mark-on-capitol-hill/

Clay Wild: exclusive interview with Anita Bartholomew

Trump tweet: https://www.thetrumparchive.com/

Giuliani "trial by combat" speech: https://www.rev.com/blog/transcripts/rudy-giuliani-speech-transcript-at-trumps-washington-d-c-rally-wants-trial-by-combat

Congresswoman Frederica Wilson: https://19thnews.org/2021/03/frederica-wilson-capitol-riot/

Early crowds gathering at Capitol: https://www.washingtonpost.com/graphics/2021/national/national-security/capitol-response-timeline

/?itid=hp-top-table-main-0106

Proud Boys adopt "Stand Back, Stand By" for their logo: https://www.
newsweek.com/proud-boys-stand-trump-debate-1535240

Alexandra Ocasio-Cortez: https://www.instagram.com/tv/CKxlyx4g-
Yb/?utm_source=ig_embed&ig_rid=9db943fb-25fd-434b-93be-84bd
463cb779 *and* https://www.youtube.com/watch?v=ffI3IPgFnSk

Trump film before speech: https://vimeo.com/508134765

Trump speech, January 6th: https://www.wsj.com/video/trump-full-s
peech-at-dc-rally-on-jan-6/E4E7BBBF-23B1-4401-ADCE-7D4432D
07030.html

Enrique Tarrio arrested: https://www.theguardian.com/world/2021/
jan/04/enrique-tarrio-rightwing-proud-boys-arrested

Proud Boys encrypted messages re plans before/after Tarrio arrest:
United States v. Ethan Nordean, Joseph Biggs, Zachary Rehl, Enrique
Tarrio, Dominic Pezzola, case #21-cr-175 Third Superseding Indict-
ment

"Pinochet did nothing wrong" t-shirt: https://www.splcenter.org/files
/proudboyssellingpinochetjpeg

Pipe bomb found: https://www.fbi.gov/wanted/seeking-info/suspect
ed-pipe-bombs-in-washington-dc *and* https://www.pbs.org/newshou
r/nation/a-year-after-jan-6-fbi-still-hunting-for-pipe-bomber-and-o
ther-insurrection-suspects

Molotov cocktails in truck: https://www.justice.gov/usao-dc/pr/al
abama-man-charged-possession-eleven-molotov-cocktails-found-n
ear-protest-us-capitol *and* United States v. Lonnie Leroy Coffman,
Statement of Offense case # 1:21-cr-00004

Alexandra Ocasio-Cortez: Alexandra Ocasio-Cortez: https://www.in
stagram.com/tv/CKxlyx4g-Yb/?utm_source=ig_embed&ig_rid=9db9
43fb-25fd-434b-93be-84bd463cb779 *and* https://www.youtube.com/
watch?v=ffI3IPgFnSk *and* https://www.youtube.com/watch?v=lU0J4
_gKszQ

Gallows "this is art": https://www.youtube.com/watch?v=9hph5KkY
w4E

David Nicholas Dempsey at gallows: Criminal Complaint, United
States of America v. David Nicholas Dempsey

Proud Boys at barricades; Ryan Samsel speaks to Joe Biggs: https://w
ww.nytimes.com/video/us/politics/100000007606996/capitol-riot-t
rump-supporters.html

Ryan Samsel's history of violence toward women: https://www.inquir
er.com/news/ryan-samsel-capitol-riot-bucks-county-pennsylvania-b
eating-20210604.html *and* https://www.mcall.com/news/breaking/m
c-capitol-riot-bucks-violence-against-women-20210602-6mn5prmgl
5ffdgqyhrisemfoja-story.html

Samsel and Johnson attack at barricades: Statement of Facts/FBI
affidavit Paul Russell Johnson, and Criminal Complaint, United States
of America v. Ryan Samsel *and* [video of attack] https://twitter.com/E
lijahSchaffer/status/1346966514990149639?ref_src=twsrc%5Etfw%7

Ctwcamp%5Etweetembed%7Ctwterm%5E1346966514990149639%7
Ctwgr%5E%7Ctwcon%5Es1_&ref_url=https%3A%2F%2Fwww.buzzf
eednews.com%2Farticle%2Fbenking%2Fcapitol-dc-riot-trump

Capitol Police Officer Carolyn Edwards: https://www.nytimes.com/2
022/01/04/magazine/jan-6-capitol-police-officers.html

Sources: Breach

Epigraph: Rioter shouting as he storms Capitol: https://www.youtub
e.com/watch?v=Xm0gPe4MgS0&t=621s

Mob storms past barricades: https://www.youtube.com/watch?v=ib
WJO02nNsY

Dominic Pezzola: Complaint with Arrest Warrant/Affidavit In Support
of A Criminal Complaint, and Government's Memorandum in Support
of Pre-Trial Detention, United States of America v. Dominic Pezzola,
case # 1:21-mj-00047 *and* https://www.nytimes.com/2021/01/13/ny
region/capitol-rioter-new-york.html

Sund suspects that pipe bombs set as diversion for siege: Police Chief
Sund February 2, 2021 letter to Nancy Pelosi on intelligence failures.

Lt. Colonel told MPD, "...here to scout out where they're going to be
when they get here." https://www.defenseone.com/policy/2021/03/d
c-guard-commander-says-unusual-restrictions-prevented-swift-resp
onse-capitol-riot/172435/

The Harder Right: An Analysis of a Recent DoD Inspector General

Investigation and Other Matters by Colonel Earl G. Matthews, U.S. Army December 1, 2021

MPD—video and radio traffic: https://www.nytimes.com/video/us/1 00000007655234/weve-lost-the-line-radio-traffic-reveals-police-un der-siege-at-capitol.html

Stinger balls used vs Black Lives Matter protesters, Lafayette Square: https://www.wusa9.com/article/news/investigations/tear-gas-grena des-washington-dc-protests-st-johns-church-lafayette-square/65-12 6bad2b-7aa3-4fe7-aae6-890fbe0383ed

Senate testimony re January 6 on February 23, 2021: Sund, Contee, Irving, Stenger: https://www.rev.com/blog/transcripts/senate-hearin g-on-january-6-capitol-attack-transcript-february-23

Trump speech, Save America rally, January 6, 2021

Ryan Nichols rescues dogs, people; appears on Ellen DeGeneres: https://www.nbcnews.com/news/weather/animal-rescuers-floren ce-dogs-saved-submerged-crate-other-pets-shuttled-n910181 *and* https://www.wect.com/story/39181544/man-who-rescued-people-a nimals-from-hurricane-honored-on-ellen/

Ryan Nichols, January 6th: https://twitter.com/TomDreisbach/status/ 1489760864135614467?ref_src=twsrc%5Etfw%7Ctwcamp%5Etweet embed%7Ctwterm%5E1489760864135614467%7Ctwgr%5E%7Ctwc on%5Es1_&ref_url=https%3A%2F%2Fwww.insider.com%2Fnew-foo tage-shows-a-capitol-rioter-screaming-threats-about-election-2022- 2 *and* Government's Opposition To Defendant's Motion For Release From Pretrial Detention, United States Of America v. Ryan Nichols, case# 21-cr-117 (TFH)

Scott Fairlamb: https://conandaily.com/2021/01/25/scott-kevin-fair
lamb-biography-13-things-about-us-capitol-riot-suspect-from-stoc
kholm-new-jersey/ *and* Criminal Complaint; Statement of Offense,
United States Of America v. Kevin Scott Fairlamb, Defendant, Case
1:21-cr-00120-RCL

Rioters climbing walls: https://www.washingtonpost.com/video/opi
nions/how-the-capitol-attack-unfolded-from-inside-trumps-rally-to-
the-riot-opinion/2021/01/12/a7146251-b076-426e-a2e3-8b503692c
89d_video.html

Rioters attacking cops, waving flags: https://www.youtube.com/watc
h?v=YzxvVi8wkrU *and* https://projects.propublica.org/parler-capitol
-videos/

Cops forced back into building: https://www.nytimes.com/video/us/
100000007655234/weve-lost-the-line-radio-traffic-reveals-police-u
nder-siege-at-capitol.html

Workers, contractors, say Trump cheated them out of money owed:
https://www.usatoday.com/story/news/politics/elections/2016/06/0
9/donald-trump-unpaid-bills-republican-president-laswuits/852972
74/

Washington Post fact-checker, Trump's 30,000+ lies: https://www.wa
shingtonpost.com/politics/2021/01/24/trumps-false-or-misleading-
claims-total-30573-over-four-years/

Trump accused of rape, other sexual misconduct: https://abcnews.go.

com/Politics/list-trumps-accusers-allegations-sexual-misconduct/sto
ry?id=51956410

Ivana Trump accused Trump of rape in divorce deposition: https://w
ww.newyorker.com/magazine/2016/10/24/documenting-trumps-ab
use-of-women

Trump suggests Obama not born in US: https://abcnews.go.com/Polit
ics/67-times-donald-trump-tweeted-birther-movement/story?id=42
145590

Trump calls Mexican immigrants criminals and rapists: https://www.
washingtonpost.com/news/the-fix/wp/2017/06/16/theyre-rapists-p
residents-trump-campaign-launch-speech-two-years-later-annotated
/

Trump calls neo-Nazis at march "very fine people" https://www.nyti
mes.com/2017/08/15/us/politics/trump-charlottesville-white-natio
nalists.html

Trump winks/nods at white supremacists: https://fortune.com/longf
orm/donald-trump-white-supremacist-genocide/

QAnon beliefs: https://theconversation.com/how-qanon-uses-satanic
-rhetoric-to-set-up-a-narrative-of-good-vs-evil-146281*and* https://e
n.wikipedia.org/wiki/QAnon

Trump claims reports of Biden's win are fake news: https://apnews.co
m/article/donald-trump-tweets-he-won-not-conceding-9ce22e9dc9
0577f7365d150c151a91c7

QAnon believers on the "storm": Trump to arrest, execute "deep state" operatives: https://www.washingtonpost.com/technology/2021/01/13/qanon-capitol-siege-trump/ *and* https://www.nytimes.com/2020/08/25/opinion/trump-qanon-birchers.html

Congresswoman Wild in House gallery: exclusive interview with Anita Bartholomew

VP Mike Pence arrives at House for joint session to certify electoral ballots: https://twitter.com/january6thcmte/status/1479151862406385671

Speeches and comments on House floor: Congressional Record-House, Proceedings and Debates of the 117th Congress, First Session, Vol. 167, No. 4, January 6, 2021

Congresswoman Boebert encouraged her restaurant staff to open-carry: https://www.denverpost.com/2018/06/22/shooters-grill-rifle-waitresses-guns/

Boebert promotes QAnon conspiracy theory: https://coloradotimesrecorder.com/2021/03/promoting-qanon-linked-conspiracy-boebert-says-resignations-will-soon-allow-gop-to-control-congress/35257/

"Today is 1776" Congresswoman Boebert tweet: https://twitter.com/laurenboebert/status/1346811381878845442?ref_src=twsrc%5Etfw

Patrick Cunnane: exclusive interview with Anita Bartholomew

Man in MAGA hat peels away netting around Capitol grounds: https://www.youtube.com/watch?v=YzxvVi8wkrU

Glover/MPD: https://www.nytimes.com/video/us/10000000765523
4/weve-lost-the-line-radio-traffic-reveals-police-under-siege-at-capi
tol.html

Officer Daniel Hodges: January 6 House Select Committee Hearing
Investigation Day 1 *and* https://www.youtube.com/watch?v=FmAx7t
2zF0g *and* HBO documentary: Four Hours at The Capitol.

Senate aides learn that National Guard hasn't been called in: https://w
ww.nytimes.com/2021/02/21/us/politics/capitol-riot-security-delay
s.html

Man tries to break window, east side Capitol; cops exhausted expressions: https://www.youtube.com/watch?v=jWJVMoe7OY0

Rioters outnumber cops almost 60 to 1: https://www.washingtonpost.
com/investigations/interactive/2021/dc-police-records-capitol-riot/

Rioters up scaffolding and into Capitol: https://www.youtube.com/w
atch?v=Xm0gPe4MgS0&t=621s

Pezzola breaks window with shield; rioters stream through: https://w
ww.youtube.com/watch?v=jtPmi4BShNM

Joe Biggs: "This is awesome": https://www.dailymail.co.uk/video/ne
ws/video-2336154/Video-awesome-says-Proud-Boys-leader-Joe-Big
gs-Capitol-riot.html

Security footage from inside (presented at impeachment trial, February
10, 2021): man carrying Confederate flag, men kicking door from
inside, second window broken, horde swarming in: https://www.yout

ube.com/watch?v=0vzeTgm2qWw

Sources: Trapped

Epigraph: rioters trying to break into House through Speakers Lobby door: https://www.youtube.com/watch?v=Xm0gPe4MgS0&t=621s

Rioters break window 2:11 pm; Secret Service moves Pence to office, 2:13 pm https://www.washingtonpost.com/politics/pence-rioters-ca pitol-attack/2021/01/15/ab62e434-567c-11eb-a08b-f1381ef3d207_s tory.html

Senator Romney: "This is what you've gotten, guys." https://twitter.co m/sabrinasiddiqui/status/1346911891197550602

Senator Lankford's truncated objection speech: Congressional Record-Senate, Proceedings and Debates of the 117th Congress, First Session, Vol. 167, No. 4, January 6, 2021

Congresswoman Torres: https://19thnews.org/2021/03/norma-torre s-capitol-riot/

Congresswoman Wild: exclusive interview with Anita Bartholomew

Keith Stern: https://www.newyorker.com/magazine/2021/01/18/as-told-to-the-pelosi-staffer-keith-stern-on-the-breach-of-the-capitol

Congressman McGovern: https://www.c-span.org/video/?513526-1/ january-6-views-house-representatives-jim-mcgovern-susan-wild

Crypt attack on cops: https://www.youtube.com/watch?v=Xm0gPe4
MgS0&t=621s and The United States District Court For The District
Of Columbia, James Blassingame and Sidney Hemby v. Donald J.
Trump, Complaint, Case 1:21-cv-00858

Contee and Sund: Senate Oversight Committee testimony: https://w
ww.rev.com/blog/transcripts/senate-hearing-on-january-6-capitol-a
ttack-transcript-february-23

Congressman Phillips: https://www.c-span.org/video/?513525-1/jan
uary-6-views-house-representatives-jamie-raskin-brian-fitzpatrick-d
ean-phillips

Congressman Malinowski: https://www.c-span.org/video/?513522-1
/january-6-views-house

Congressman Crow: https://www.c-span.org/video/?513522-1/janu
ary-6-views-house *and* https://www.rollingstone.com/politics/politic
s-news/jason-crow-capitol-attack-mob-january-6-1111073/

Congressman Mullin: https://www.c-span.org/video/?513522-1/jan
uary-6-views-house

Congresswoman Dean: https://www.c-span.org/video/?513523-1/
january-6-views-house-representatives-zoe-lofgren-rodney-davis-
madeleine-dean *and* Patrick Cunnane exclusive interview with Anita
Bartholomew

Rioters outside House chamber/speakers lobby: https://www.youtub
e.com/watch?v=Xm0gPe4MgS0&t=621s

Ashley Babbit background: https://www.washingtonpost.com/local/
public-safety/ashli-babbitt-capitol-shooting/2021/01/07/c28bb0ac-5
116-11eb-b96e-0e54447b23a1_story.html *and* https://apnews.com/a
rticle/donald-trump-us-news-shootings-san-diego-veterans-e8c7563
ff4cce671a2b52a8e7645945c *and* https://www.nytimes.com/2021/01
/08/us/who-was-ashli-babbitt.html

Congressional reps escape as rioters try to get to them: Congressional
Record Volume 167, Number 25, Senate, Wednesday, February 10,
2021, Trial Of Donald J. Trump, President Of The United States *and*
https://www.c-span.org/video/?513526-1/january-6-views-house-re
presentatives-jim-mcgovern-susan-wild *and* https://www.youtube.co
m/watch?v=jWJVMoe7OY0

Rioters' attempts to break down door/shooting of Ashli Babbit:
https://www.youtube.com/watch?v=Xm0gPe4MgS0&t=621s *and*
https://www.youtube.com/watch?v=PfiS8MsfSF4

Adrienne Wild: Exclusive interview with Anita Bartholomew

Clay Wild: Exclusive interview with Anita Bartholomew

2,000 to 2,500 rioters entered Capitol building per DoJ: https://www.
npr.org/2022/01/06/1070736018/jan-6-anniversary-investigation-c
ases-defendants-justice

Sources: Meanwhile, In The Senate

Epigraph: Senator Schumer's remarks upon reconvening Senate,
January 6, 2021: https://www.democrats.senate.gov/news/press-r
eleases/schumer-floor-remarks-upon-the-reconvening-of-the-united

-states-senate-after-failed-insurrection-by-violent-pro-trump-mob

Senate sealed 2:15 pm: https://www.washingtonpost.com/politics/in side-capitol-siege/2021/01/09/e3ad3274-5283-11eb-bda4-615aaefd 0555_story.html

Officer Goodman: https://www.washingtonpost.com/local/public-sa fety/goodman-capitol-police-video/2021/01/13/08ab3eb6-546b-11e b-a931-5b162d0d033d_story.html *and* https://www.washingtonpost. com/politics/pence-rioters-capitol-attack/2021/01/15/ab62e434-56 7c-11eb-a08b-f1381ef3d207_story.html *and* https://www.youtube.co m/watch?v=quTbyIV4h7M&t=176s

Doug Jensen: United States v. Jensen, case # 1:21-cr-00006, District Court, District of Columbia

Jacob Chansley/QAnon shaman: United States v. Chansley, case #2:21-mj-05000, District Court, D. Arizona *and* https://www.youtube.com/ watch?v=jWJVMoe7OY0

Three percenters: https://en.wikipedia.org/wiki/Three_Percenters

QAnon: https://www.bbc.com/news/53498434

Robert Gieswein: Memorandum Opinion—Motion Denied for Pre-Trial Release, United States v. Robert Gieswein, case # 2021-0024,

Affidavit in Support of A Criminal Complaint, United States v. Pezzola, case 121-mj-00047

Insurgents, including Pezzola, forced out by police through same

window Pezzola broke: https://www.buzzfeednews.com/article/z
oetillman/capitol-footage-lawsuit-release-insurrection

Trump tweet: https://www.thetrumparchive.com/

Pence evacuates Senate office for secure location: Congressional
Record Volume 167, Number 25, Senate, Wednesday, February 10,
2021, Trial Of Donald J. Trump, President Of The United States *and*
https://www.wusa9.com/article/news/national/capitol-riots/vp-pen
ce-hunkered-down-in-underground-loading-dock-for-hours-on-jan-
6-witness-testifies-couy-griffin-cowboys-for-trump/65-90384ca0-6
0df-4b8a-a21c-610cc5f78604

Senator Lee attempts to help overturn election (texts between Mike
Lee and Mark Meadows): https://www.cnn.com/2022/04/15/politics
/read-mark-meadows-texts-mike-lee-chip-roy/index.html

Senator Lee call with Trump: https://www.sltrib.com/news/politics/
2021/02/11/what-sen-mike-lee-told-me/

Tuberville background: https://www.bamapolitics.com/43646/tuber
ville-radio-ad-god-sent-us-donald-trump/ *and* https://www.cnn.com
/2020/03/10/politics/trump-endorses-tommy-tuberville-over-jeff-se
ssions-alabama-us-senate/index.html *and* https://www.alreporter.co
m/2021/01/27/photos-posts-put-tuberville-in-trumps-hotel-on-jan-
5-despite-him-denying-meeting/ *and* https://www.washingtonpost.c
om/opinions/2020/12/21/tommy-tuberville-is-making-strong-bid-b
ecome-senates-dimmest-member/

Senator Tuberville call with Trump: https://www.cnn.com/2021/01/
08/politics/mike-lee-tommy-tuberville-trump-misdialed-capitol-riot

/index.html

Trump to Pence: either patriot or pussy: https://www.rollingstone.co
m/politics/politics-news/trump-pence-patriot-pussy-1257669/

Luttig, Jacob, Yoo advice: https://lawandcrime.com/u-s-capitol-siege/
these-are-the-lawyers-who-told-mike-pence-that-despite-trumps-pr
essure-campaign-vp-had-no-power-to-overturn-election-results/

Yoo's defense of torture: Memorandum for William J. Haynes II, General Counsel of the Department of Defense re: Military Interrogation of Alien Unlawful Combatants Held Outside the United States, March 14, 2003; and of warrantless spying: Letter to District Judge Colleen Kollar-Kotelly, May 17, 2022

Eastman pressures Pence's counsel: Select Committee To Investigate The January 6th Attack On The U.S. Capitol, U.S. House Of Representatives, Washington, D.C., Deposition of Greg Jacob, February 1,2022, and Deposition of John Eastman, December 9, 2021

DeGrave (with Sandlin and Colt) broke through doors, overpowered police: Opinion on Pre-Trial Detention, United States v. Degrave, case # 2021-0090 (D.D.C. 2021) *and* https://lawandcrime.com/u-s-capitol-breach/there-is-going-to-be-violence-man-seen-smoking-joint-inside-u-s-capitol-allegedly-discussed-shipping-guns-called-jan-6-the-boogaloo/

Rioters including DeGrave, Sandlin, Colt reach Senate gallery, find senators gone: https://www.youtube.com/watch?v=270F8s5TEKY

Jessica Watkins/Oath Keepers in stack formation: https://www.youtu

be.com/watch?v=p1QJLffN15k

Exhibit 5, Rhodes' Open Letter to Trump re Insurrection Act, calling up militia; Oath Keepers do not appear to have planned to storm Capitol, Exhibit 6 instant messaging app texts; and Stewart Rhodes, on instant messaging app, refutes some Oath Keepers belief that antifa stormed the Capitol, United States Of America v. Elmer Stewart Rhodes, Kelly Meggs, Kenneth Harrelson, Jessica Watkins, Joshua James, Roberto Minuta, Joseph Hackett, David Moerschel, Brian Ulrich, Thomas Caldwell and Edward Vallejo, Defendants—texts, Exhibit 6, case # 1:22-cr-00015-APM

Jessica Watkins: https://www.daytondailynews.com/crime/capitol -riot-prosecutors-say-champaign-county-womans-training-includ ed-war-games/RE5YX5MNW5AY5IRE2QIUSJNRUY/ *and* Jessica Watkin's Motion For Release To Home Confinement Pending The Outcome Of Her Case; Government's Opposition to Defendant's Motion To Reconsider Detention, United States of America v. Jessica Watkins, Case # 1:21-cr-28 (APM); *and* video Watkins, other Oath Keepers, trying to force their way into Senate: https://twitter.com/trb rtc/status/1373032386720636928?s=20 *and* https://www.buzzfeedne ws.com/article/jessicagarrison/conspiracy-charge-ohio-militia-capit ol?bfsource=relatedmanual

Insurrection Act: https://www.law.cornell.edu/uscode/text/10/251; https://www.law.cornell.edu/uscode/text/10/252; https://www.law. cornell.edu/uscode/text/10/253

Thomas Caldwell: Amended Criminal Complaint, United States of America vs Jessica Marie Watkins, Donovan Ray Crowl, Thomas Edward Caldwell, case # 1:21-mj-00119 *and* https://www.washington

post.com/local/legal-issues/thomas-caldwell-capitol-riot-detention/
2021/02/11/a94bb3f2-6c92-11eb-9f80-3d7646ce1bc0_story.html

Stewart Rhodes: "We're concerned about a Benghazi style attack..."
https://tv.infowars.com/index/display/id/11028

Obama ends Don't Ask, Don't Tell: https://obamawhitehouse.archives
.gov/blog/2012/09/20/archives-end-dont-ask-dont-tell

Trump reinstates ban on trans service members: https://www.theguar
dian.com/us-news/2019/apr/12/transgender-ban-military-trump-ta
ke-effect-dont-ask-dont-tell

Lily Stein, Jewish woman, spied for Nazis: *Double Agent* by Peter Duffy,
Scribner 2014

Supreme Court Justice Clarence Thomas on school desegregation:
https://www.nytimes.com/1995/07/02/weekinreview/the-nation-ga
vel-rousers-on-race-it-s-thomas-v-an-old-ideal.html

Rioters in senate, QAnon Shaman chanting/praying, Black, Brock,
Officer Keith Robishaw, yellow plaid shirt guy: https://www.youtube.
com/watch?v=270F8s5TEKY

Josiah Colt in Pence's chair yelling "Trump won that election" https://t
witter.com/igorbobic/status/1346906369232920576/photo/1

Joshua Black: Affidavit in Support of Criminal Complaint and Arrest
Warrant; Memorandum In Support Of Pretrial Detention United States
vs Joshua Matthew Black case # 2:21-mj-00010 *and* https://www.al.co
m/news/2021/01/joshua-black-alabama-man-arrested-for-storming-

capitol-says-he-was-shot-in-face-while-defending-police.html

Larry Brock: Affidavit In Support Of Criminal Complaint And Arrest Warrant United States vs Larry Rendall Brock; United States' Response To Defendant's Motion To Reconsider Electronic Monitoring Or In The Alternative To Modify Certain Restrictions On Travel, United States vs Larry Rendall Brock, case #. 1:21-CR-140-JDB

Acting Defense Secretary Miller "activates" but doesn't deploy Guard; Guard awaits order that doesn't come: https://www.justsecurity.org/76117/the-official-and-unofficial-timeline-of-defense-department-actions-on-january-6/

Sources: Last Stand on the Lower West Terrace

Epigraph: President Joe Biden, January 6, 2022, commemorating the first anniversary of the insurrection

Officer Hodges: Full January 6th Select Committee hearing with officers' testimony and video: https://www.c-span.org/video/?513434-1/capitol-dc-police-testify-january-6-attack&live&vod&start=60 *and* HBO documentary: Four Hours at The Capitol *and* Press conference, Officer Hodges: https://www.youtube.com/watch?v=FmAx7t2zF0g

Danny Rodriguez: Exhibit A, Interview of Daniel "D.J." Rodriguez, Wednesday March 31, 2021, United States v. Daniel Rodriguez, case # 1:21-cr-00246-ABJ

Sergeant Gonell: https://www.cnn.com/2021/06/03/politics/capitol-police-officers-exclusive-interview-january-6/index.html *and* https://www.washingtonpost.com/local/public-safety/capitol-riot-p

olice-injuries-trauma/2021/07/23/e008f0f0-d8d8-11eb-9bbb-37c3
0dcf9363_story.html *and* Full January 6th Select Committee hearing
with officers' testimony and video: https://www.c-span.org/video/?5
13434-1/capitol-dc-police-testify-january-6-attack&live&vod&start=
60 *and* HBO documentary: Four Hours at The Capitol *and* https://ww
w.washingtonpost.com/local/public-safety/capitol-riot-police-injurie
s-trauma/2021/07/23/e008f0f0-d8d8-11eb-9bbb-37c30dcf9363_sto
ry.html

Rioter with asthma: Complaint with Arrest warrant, John Steven
Anderson, case 1:21 MJ-00239

Officer Hodges and other officers' attackers, including Patrick Mc-
Caughey (pinned Hodges with shield) and Steven Cappuccio (stole
baton; pulled off gas mask): Fourth Superseding Indictment; also
Government's Opposition to Defendant's Motion for Pre-Trial Re-
lease, Geoffrey Sills; also Pre-Trial Detention Memorandum Opinion,
Federico Guillermo Klein; United States v. Patrick E. McCaughey
III, Tristan Chandler Stevens, David Lee Judd, Christopher Joseph
Quaglin, Robert Morss, Geoffrey William Sills, David Mehaffie, Steven
Cappuccio, and Federico Guillermo Klein case # 1:21-cr-00040-TNM
and https://www.wusa9.com/article/news/national/capitol-riots/pat
rick-mccaughey-capitol-riot-charge-assault-crush-officer-daniel-hod
ges-breach-insurrection/65-3f9ab870-0915-41ce-8b6f-8991a72d82a
d *and* https://www.huffpost.com/entry/capitol-riot-stripes-guy-char
ged-officer-daniel-hodges-attack_n_6115bb42e4b07c14031319fd?9z
and https://www.justice.gov/usao-dc/defendants/cappuccio-steven

Rioter who tried to drag Gonell out of tunnel: Memorandum Denying
Defendant's Motion To Revoke Detention Order and For Pretrial
Release, United States v. Kyle Fitzsimons, case # 21-cr-158

Officers Mike Fanone and Jimmy Albright: Full January 6th Select Committee hearing with officers' testimony and video: https://www.c-span.org/video/?513434-1/capitol-dc-police-testify-january-6-attack&live&vod&start=60 *and* HBO documentary: Four Hours at The Capitol *and* https://time.com/6087577/michael-fanone-january-6-interview/ *and* https://www.wusa9.com/article/features/producers-picks/dc-police-officer-describes-fighting-for-his-life-as-rioters-dragged-him/65-5405dfde-6c19-4c99-9160-e8a3d4173987 *and* https://buffalonews.com/news/local/d-c-officer-details-alleged-attack-by-amherst-man-others/article_bbd72f24-eee7-11eb-a801-33ae2c498520.html *and* https://www.washingtonpost.com/local/public-safety/capitol-riot-police-injuries-trauma/2021/07/23/e008f0f0-d8d8-11eb-9bbb-37c30dcf9363_story.html

(Sibick stole Fanone's radio, badge, and ammunition; Young tried to steal Fanone's gun): Grand Jury Indictment, also Sibick Statement of Facts, United States v. Thomas F. Sibick, Albuquerque Cosper Head, and Kyle J. Young case # 1:21-cr-00291

4:17 pm Trump video tweet: https://www.thetrumparchive.com/

4:18 pm Miller deploys Guard: https://www.justsecurity.org/76117/the-official-and-unofficial-timeline-of-defense-department-actions-on-january-6/

Ryan Nichols: Government's Opposition To Defendant's Motion For Release From Pretrial Detention, United States Of America v. Ryan Nichols, case# 21-cr-117 (TFH)

Geoffrey Sills (Stole officer's baton and beat cops with it): Government's Opposition to Defendant's Motion for Pre-Trial Release, United

States v. Geoffrey Sills, case # 1:21-cr-00040-TNM

David Nicholas Dempsey climbed on backs of other rioters to attack officers: Criminal Complaint, United States of America v. David Nicholas Dempsey

Mattice and Mault (climbed on backs of other rioters to attack officers): Criminal complaint: United States v Cody Mattice, James Phillip Mault, case # 1:21-mj-00622-ZMF

Crutch attack: Memorandum Opinion, United States v. Jack Wade Whitton, case # 21-35-5

Attacked cops with fire extinguisher, Complaint, United States v. Robert S. Palmer, case # 1:21-mj-00301

Attacked cops with table leg: Statement of Facts, United States v. Timothy Des Jardin, case # 1:21-mj-00663

Pepper spray attack: Memorandum Opinion, United States v. Jeffrey Scott Brown, case # 21-mj-565 (ZMF)

Officer Dunn: Full January 6th Select Committee hearing with officers' testimony and video: https://www.c-span.org/video/?513434-1/c apitol-dc-police-testify-january-6-attack&live&vod&start=60 *and* https://www.washingtonpost.com/local/public-safety/capitol-riot-p olice-injuries-trauma/2021/07/23/e008f0f0-d8d8-11eb-9bbb-37c30 dcf9363_story.html

Roseanne Boyland: https://www.washingtonpost.com/dc-md-va /interactive/2021/wayfair-qanon-sex-trafficking-conspiracy/ *and* https://www.nytimes.com/2021/01/15/us/rosanne-boyland-capitol-riot-death.html

Officer Sicknick: https://www.nytimes.com/2022/01/04/magazine/jan-6-capitol-police-officers.html

Sources: Aftermath

Epigraph: Liz Cheney quote from WSJ op-ed https://cheney.house.gov/2022/02/11/congresswoman-liz-cheney-newsletter-february-11th/

Pelosi, McConnell evacuated to Fort McNair: https://www.cnn.com/2021/01/06/politics/us-capitol-lockdown/index.html

Pence and family, underground garage: https://www.newsweek.com/mike-pence-january-6-riot-loading-dock-underground-parking-garage-1647353

Pence back on dais 8:06 pm January 6; applause; objections in Senate: Congressional Record-Senate, Proceedings and Debates of the 117th Congress, First Session, Vol. 167, No. 4, January 6, 2021

Congresswoman Wilson: https://19thnews.org/2021/03/frederica-wilson-capitol-riot/

House gaveled in at 9:02 pm; objections: Congressional Record-House, Proceedings and Debates of the 117th Congress, First Session, Vol. 167, No. 4, January 6, 2021

Greg Pence, VP's brother, votes to object to PA certification: https://www.therepublic.com/2021/01/08/rep-greg-pence-votes-to-object-to-pennsylvania-electoral-college-results/

Congressman Clyde claims there was "no insurrection" and looked like a "normal tourist visit." https://www.washingtonpost.com/politic s/2021/05/18/clyde-tourist-capitol-riot-photos/

Photo of Congressman Clyde appearing to scream in panic as insur-rectionists break glass of House chamber door: https://twitter.com/br yrsmith/status/1394470243544838151?ref_src=twsrc%5Etfw%7Ctw camp%5Etweetembed%7Ctwterm%5E1394470243544838151%7Ctw gr%5E%7Ctwcon%5Es1_&ref_url=https%3A%2F%2Fwww.washingto npost.com%2Fpolitics%2F2021%2F05%2F18%2Fclyde-tourist-capitol -riot-photos%2F

Chao and DeVos resign: https://www.washingtonpost.com/politics/2 021/01/08/daily-202-elaine-chao-betsy-devos-resign-after-standing-by-trump-almost-four-years/

Other resignations after coup attempt: https://www.nytimes.com/art icle/trump-resignations.html

Speaker Pelosi feared Trump would launch nukes: https://www.washi ngtonpost.com/national-security/pelosi-trump-nuclear-codes/2021/ 01/08/032d95ac-51e0-11eb-bda4-615aaefd0555_story.html

VP Pence says no to invoking 25th; resolution to impeach Trump: https://www.cbsnews.com/live-updates/trump-25th-amendment-ho use-pence/

House Minority Leader McCarthy against impeachment; suggests censure: https://www.c-span.org/video/?c4937290/gop-leader-mcca

rthy-president-trump-bears-responsibility-capitol-attack-favors-cen
sure

Senate Minority Leader McConnell condemns Trump after voting to acquit: Trial of Donald J. Trump, President of the United States, Congressional Record-Senate, Proceedings and Debates of the 117th Congress, Vol. 167, No. 28, February 13, 2021

30,000 National Guard troops sent to Capitol after Jan 6 fencing with razor wire: https://www.washingtonpost.com/local/national-guard-capitol-deployment/2021/03/31/6a616980-8fe6-11eb-a74e-1f4cf89f d948_story.html

Former acting Defense Secretary Miller testimony: Hearing Before The Committee On Oversight And Reform House Of Representatives 117th Congress First Session May 12, 2021 –Christopher Miller testimony

Walker "All military commanders normally have immediate response authority to protect property, life, and in my case, federal functions — federal property and life" but Miller rescinded his authority: https://w ww.washingtonpost.com/national-security/dc-guard-capitol-riots-w illiam-walker-pentagon/2021/01/26/98879f44-5f69-11eb-ac8f-4ae0 5557196e_story.html

Trump wanted National Guard to protect pro-Trump people: https://w ww.politico.com/news/2021/12/12/meadows-jan-6-national-guard-trump-524133

Recommendation to invoke martial law and have the secretary of defense seize voting machines: Draft Executive Order, author unattributed, December 16, 2020; December 18th meeting about above draft order: https://www.axios.com/trump-oval-office-meeting-sidn ey-powell-a8e1e466-2e42-42d0-9cf1-26eb267f8723.html

Senate Republicans block formation of January 6th commission: https://www.npr.org/2021/05/28/1000524897/senate-republica ns-block-plan-for-independent-commission-on-jan-6-capitol-riot

Minority Leader McCarthy attempt to place Congressmen Jordan and Banks, who signed onto a lawsuit to overturn PA's electoral votes, on House Select Committee to investigate January 6th. https://www.cnn. com/2021/07/19/politics/house-republicans-chosen-for-january-6-c ommittee/index.html

Speaker Pelosi vetoes Congressmen Banks and Jordan: https://www.p olitico.com/news/2021/07/21/pelosi-vetoes-banks-jordan-for-jan-6- select-committee-500424

Congresswoman Cheney ousted as conference chair: https://www.np r.org/2021/05/12/995072539/gop-poised-to-oust-cheney-from-lead ership-over-her-criticism-of-trump

January 6th House Select Committee hearing: https://www.youtube.c om/watch?v=vHrt44ANHIA

850 MPD officers deployed to Capitol and two officers committed suicide: https://www.washingtonpost.com/local/public-safety/conte e-dcpolice-capitol-riot-/2021/01/26/8f386d12-6020-11eb-9061-07a bcc1f9229_story.html

Approximately 1,000 assaults on police: https://abcnews.go.com/US/ approximately-1000-assaults-law-enforcement-occurred-capitol-atta ck/story?id=79793226

140 officers injured: https://www.washingtonpost.com/local/public-safety/police-union-says-140-officers-injured-in-capitol-riot/2021/01/27/60743642-60e2-11eb-9430-e7c77b5b0297_story.html

January 6th committee interviewed Ivanka Trump, Jared Kushner, 800 witnesses in all: https://www.mercurynews.com/2022/04/05/source-ivanka-trump-to-testify-before-jan-6-panel/

Mark Meadows texts to January 6th committee, including with Ginni Thomas: https://www.vanityfair.com/news/2022/03/january-6-committee-ginni-thomas

Trump allies refuse to cooperate with committee: https://www.pbs.org/newshour/politics/jan-6-committee-votes-to-hold-trump-advisers-scavino-navarro-in-contempt

Doug Jensen: https://www.desmoinesregister.com/story/news/crime-and-courts/2022/01/12/capitol-riot-iowa-suspect-doug-jensen-denied-pretrial-release-january-6-trump-arrests/9187021002/

Jacob Chansley/QAnon shaman sentenced to 41 months: https://www.pbs.org/newshour/nation/jan-6-rioter-known-as-qanon-shaman-sentenced-to-41-months

Lonnie Leroy Coffman sentenced to 46 months: https://www.cnn.com/2022/04/01/politics/lonnie-coffman-capitol-riot/index.html *and* United States v. Lonnie Leroy Coffman, Statement of Offense case # 1:21-cr-00004

Jessica Watkins, Stewart Rhodes, other Oath Keepers charged with seditious conspiracy: https://www.justice.gov/opa/pr/leader-oath-ke epers-and-10-other-individuals-indicted-federal-court-seditious-con spiracy-and

Proud Boys charged with seditious conspiracy: United States v. Ethan Nordean, Joseph Biggs, Zachary Rehl, Enrique Tarrio, Dominic Pezzola, case #21-cr-175 Third Superseding Indictment

Ryan Nichols charges: https://www.justice.gov/usao-dc/defendants/ nichols-ryan

Danny Rodriguez charges: https://www.cbsnews.com/losangeles/ne ws/edward-badalian-daniel-rodriguez-charged-conspiracy-assault-ja n-6-capitol-breach/

Sibick asks to use dating apps while awaiting trial: https://www.wusa 9.com/article/news/national/capitol-riots/capitol-rioter-thomas-sibi ck-accused-of-robbing-officer-michael-fanone-asks-judge-to-let-hi m-use-dating-apps-january-6-donald-trump/65-c06e9e22-0e6d-438 9-b99c-39cd461155db

Sources: The Once and Future Coup

Epigraph: Order Re Privilege Of Documents Dated January 4-7, 2021, John C. Eastman Plaintiff, vs. Bennie G. Thompson, *et al.*, Defendants, case # 8:22-cv-00099-DOC-DFM

The Election That Could Break America, https://www.theatlantic.co m/magazine/archive/2020/11/what-if-trump-refuses-concede/6164 24/

Bannon: "Kill the Biden presidency…"https://www.rollingstone.com/
politics/politics-news/steve-bannon-january-6-kill-biden-presidency
-1230904/

Differing perspectives on the Independent State Legislature Doctrine:
https://www.nationalreview.com/corner/rick-hasens-misleading-acc
ount-of-the-article-ii-electors-arguments/ *and* https://electionlawblo
g.org/?p=124639 *and* https://washingtonspectator.org/road-map-for-
a-constitutional-coup/ *and* https://constitutioncenter.org/interactive-
constitution/podcast/what-is-the-independent-state-legislature-doct
rine

Bogus Trump electors from states Biden won: https://january6th.hou
se.gov/news/press-releases/select-committee-subpoenas-alternate-el
ectors-seven-states

Trump, Eastman, Giuliani lobby 300 state legislators to overturn
election: https://www.washingtonexaminer.com/washington-secrets
/exclusive-trump-urges-state-legislators-to-reject-electoral-votes-yo
u-are-the-real-power

Eastman's 6-page memo on overturning the election: "Privileged And
Confidential, January 6 scenario"

Eastman retires from Chapman, under pressure: https://www.cbsnew
s.com/losangeles/news/jan-6-committee-to-subpoena-former-chap
man-law-professor-john-eastman/

Select Committee's response to Eastman attempts to keep papers from
committee: Defendants' Memorandum Of Law, and Order Re Privilege
Of Documents Dated January 4-7, 2021, John C. Eastman Plaintiff, vs.

Bennie G. Thompson, *et al.*, Defendants, case # 8:22-cv-00099-DOC-DFM

Only 8 of Pennsylvania's 18 congressional reps (partisan breakdown is 50/50 GOP to Democrat) object to Biden's certification: https://www.inquirer.com/politics/election/electoral-college-certification-congress-pennsylvania-republicans-20210106.html

Only 3 of Michigan's 14 congressional reps (partisan breakdown is 50/50 GOP to Democrat) object to Biden's certification: https://www.mlive.com/politics/2021/01/3-michigan-republicans-object-to-electoral-votes-in-arizona-pennsylvania.html

Majority Wisconsin congressional delegation votes to certify Biden's win: https://journaltimes.com/2-wis-republicans-vote-against-election-certification-following-storming-of-the-capitol-by-trump-supporters/article_c0fbe23e-51fb-5616-8c35-2600279524d6.html

Wyoming Congresswoman Liz Cheney voted to certify and pushed back against the Big Lie: https://www.vox.com/2021/5/5/22419504/liz-cheney-trump-big-lie *and* https://twitter.com/liz_cheney/status/1346791515889262592

Jacobs/Eastman meeting re Eastman 6-page memo: https://www.politico.com/news/2022/06/11/pence-trump-jan-6-lawyer-memo-00038996

Congresswoman Cheney quoting Steve Bannon related to contempt referral "Man, if I was in a revolution...": https://twitter.com/PoliticusSarah/status/1450611084876976138?ref_src=twsrc%5Etfw%7Ctwcamp%5Etweetembed%7Ctwterm%5E1450611084876976138%7Ctwg

r%5E%7Ctwcon%5Es1_&ref_url=https%3A%2F%2Fwww.newsandgu
ts.com%2Fhouse-committee-votes-to-hold-bannon-in-contempt-of-
congress%2F

Oath Keepers expected battle with antifa: Exhibit 6 instant messaging
app texts, United States Of America v. Elmer Stewart Rhodes, Kelly
Meggs, Kenneth Harrelson, Jessica Watkins, Joshua James, Roberto
Minuta, Joseph Hackett, David Moerschel, Brian Ulrich, Thomas
Caldwell and Edward Vallejo, Defendants, case # 1:22-cr-00015-APM

Officer Fanone attacker Danny Rodiguez expected battle with antifa:
Exhibit A, Interview of Daniel "D.J." Rodriguez, Wednesday March 31,
2021, United States v. Daniel Rodriguez, case # 1:21-cr-00246-ABJ

John Sullivan of Utah, BLM supporter, provocateur, and videographer
at Capitol siege: https://www.deseret.com/utah/2021/1/7/22219733
/utah-activist-inside-u-s-capitol-says-woman-killed-was-first-to-try-
and-enter-house-chamber-sullivan

The Insurrection Act allows president to use military to put down a
rebellion: https://en.wikipedia.org/wiki/Insurrection_Act_of_1807

Martial law: https://en.wikipedia.org/wiki/Martial_law_in_the_Unit
ed_States

Ryan Grim speculation about Trump's strategy: https://theintercept.c
om/2021/02/13/trump-impeachment-republican-senators/?utm_me
dium=email&utm_source=The%20Intercept%20Newsletter

Liz Cheney says Trump supported "Hang Mike Pence" chant: https://w
ww.youtube.com/watch?v=hZ0yNe3cFx4 Trump denies saying or

even thinking this: https://www.washingtonpost.com/politics/2022/
06/10/jan6-trump-pence-deserves-hanged-cheney-capitol/

Others speculate it would have been enough to get Pence out of the
Capitol and prevent his return: https://www.msnbc.com/all-in/watc
h/new-details-on-why-pence-refused-to-get-in-secret-service-car-o
n-jan-6-138609733788

Giuliani call on Senator Lee's phone, attempting to reach Senator
Tuberville: https://thedispatch.com/p/giuliani-to-senator-try-to-just-
slow?s=r

Principled Republican officials stood up against the Big Lie: https://ww
w.newyorker.com/news/our-columnists/state-and-local-republicans-
standing-up-to-trump-are-putting-national-gop-leaders-to-shame

Restrictive new voting laws: https://www.brennancenter.org/our-wo
rk/research-reports/voting-laws-roundup-february-2022

Congressman Chabot, 2019 Politico story, What if Trump Won't
Concede? https://www.politico.com/story/2019/06/21/trump-el
ection-2020-1374589

Congressman Chabot objects to Biden certification: https://ohiocapit
aljournal.com/2021/01/07/4-ohio-congressmen-object-to-electoral-
college-count-in-effort-to-overturn-result/

Threats against Raffensperger and family; bomb threats at polling
places: https://www.reuters.com/investigates/special-report/usa-tru
mp-georgia-threats/

Threats against election workers—Trump and Giuliani call out women workers by name: https://www.reuters.com/investigates/special-report/usa-election-threats-georgia/

Threats against other election officials: https://www.reuters.com/investigates/special-report/usa-election-threats-gatewaypundit/

Threats against Michigan and Arizona secretaries of state: https://www.newsweek.com/your-days-are-f-king-numbered-threats-rained-down-election-officials-1654247

Democracy Docket/Georgia Governor Kemp: https://www.democracydocket.com/news/how-the-gop-will-try-to-subvert-our-elections/

McCarthy rebukes Trump: https://www.politico.com/news/2021/01/13/mccarthy-trump-responsibility-capitol-riot-458975

Senator Graham, 2015, Trump a "race-baiting, xenophobic, religious bigot": https://www.youtube.com/watch?v=2bkDykGhM8c

Senator Graham, 2019, Trump not racist: https://www.newsweek.com/lindsey-graham-trump-not-racist-tweets-1450060

124 generals and admirals sign letter supporting Big Lie: https://www.politico.com/news/2021/05/11/retired-brass-biden-election-487374

Three generals warn of breakdown, chain of command, in the event of a coup: https://www.washingtonpost.com/opinions/2021/12/17/eaton-taguba-anderson-generals-military/

National Popular Vote Interstate Compact: https://www.nationalpop

ularvote.com/

Trump continues rallies where he promotes Big Lie: https://www.don
aldjtrump.com/events

Experts say democracy in peril: https://www.theatlantic.
com/magazi
ne/archive/2022/01/january-6-insurrection-trump-coup-2024-electi
on/620843/

661 Billionaires Pumped $1.2 Billion Into 2020 Elections, buying
access, influencing policy: https://americansfortaxfairness.org/iss
ue/billionaires-spending-39-times-federal-elections-since-citizens-u
nited-supreme-court-decision-2010/

About the Author

I specialize in narrative—which is just another way of saying story-telling. I've written well over 100 narratives in my career, two of which were adapted into TV movies.

A longtime contributor to both the US and international editions of *Reader's Digest* (and former contributing editor to the US edition), I've also written for a number of other major magazines.

— *Anita Bartholomew*

Also by Anita Bartholomew

The Midget's House

"...the old gossip about the origins of the house did spark the idea for Anita's novel. What if the disquiet spirit of a lovely and tragic midget circus performer did inhabit the house? What if she is confused and unable to cross over to the other side until she sorts out what really happened to her? Was she murdered?

"Anita took the idea and let her imagination do the rest, constructing a plot that involves a beguiling 3-foot-tall heroine named Lucinda, the circus impresario who falls in love with her, an evil jealous character named Enid and the modern-day woman who lives in the house."

– Sarasota Herald-Tribune

Something to Prove

"No episode of "ER" or "Grey's Anatomy" could equal the drama Dr. Yvonne Thornton experienced saving the life of a young mother who couldn't stop bleeding, delivering a baby who had developed outside the womb or performing a Caesarean on a patient that required two operating tables. The prototype of today's working mother, she accomplished all of this — then raced home to be there for the piano recitals and chess tournaments of her own two children."

— Philadelphia Tribune

Grand Prize Winner of the 2011 New York Book Festival

Printed in Great Britain
by Amazon

15411082R00130